How to Be Successful in Your First Year of Teaching College:

Everything You Need to Know That They Don't Teach You in School

By Terry Webster

HOW TO BE SUCCESSFUL IN YOUR FIRST YEAR OF TEACHING
COLLEGE: EVERYTHING YOU NEED TO KNOW THAT THEY DON'T
TEACH YOU IN SCHOOL

Copyright © 2010 Atlantic Publishing Group, Inc.
1405 SW 6th Avenue • Ocala, Florida 34471 • Phone 800-814-1132 • Fax 352-622-1875
Web site: www.atlantic-pub.com • E-mail: sales@atlantic-pub.com
SAN Number: 268-1250

Library of Congress Cataloging-in-Publication Data

Webster, Terry, 1962-
  How to be successful in your first year of teaching college : everything you need to know that
they don't teach you in school / Terry Webster.
     p. cm.
  Includes bibliographical references and index.
  ISBN-13: 978-1-60138-219-1 (alk. paper)
  ISBN-10: 1-60138-219-7 (alk. paper)
  1. College teaching--Handbooks, manuals, etc. 2. First year teachers--Handbooks, manuals,
etc. I. Title.
  LB2331.W358 2010
  378.1'2--dc22
                           2010001581

Printed in the United States

PROJECT MANAGER: Nicole Orr • norr@atlantic-pub.com
PEER REVIEWER: Marilee Griffin • mgriffin@atlantic-pub.com
FINAL EDITOR: Rebecca Bentz
EDITORIAL ASSISTANT: Amy Gronauer • agronauer@atlantic-pub.com
INTERIOR DESIGN: Holly Marie Gibbs • hgibbs@atlantic-pub.com
FRONT & BACK COVER DESIGN: Jackie Miller • millerjackiej@gmail.com

Printed on Recycled Paper

We recently lost our beloved pet "Bear," who was not only our best and dearest friend but also the "Vice President of Sunshine" here at Atlantic Publishing. He did not receive a salary but worked tirelessly 24 hours a day to please his parents. Bear was a rescue dog that turned around and showered myself, my wife, Sherri, his grand-  parents Jean, Bob, and Nancy, and every person and animal he met (maybe not rabbits) with friendship and love. He made a lot of people smile every day.

We wanted you to know that a portion of the profits of this book will be donated to The Humane Society of the United States. *–Douglas & Sherri Brown*

The human-animal bond is as old as human history. We cherish our animal companions for their unconditional affection and acceptance. We feel a thrill when we glimpse wild creatures in their natural habitat or in our own backyard.

Unfortunately, the human-animal bond has at times been weakened. Humans have exploited some animal species to the point of extinction.

The Humane Society of the United States makes a difference in the lives of animals here at home and worldwide. The HSUS is dedicated to creating a world where our relationship with animals is guided by compassion. We seek a truly humane society in which animals are respected for their intrinsic value, and where the human-animal bond is strong.

Want to help animals? We have plenty of suggestions. Adopt a pet from a local shelter, join The Humane Society and be a part of our work to help companion animals and wildlife. You will be funding our educational, legislative, investigative and outreach projects in the U.S. and across the globe.

Or perhaps you'd like to make a memorial donation in honor of a pet, friend or relative? You can through our Kindred Spirits program. And if you'd like to contribute in a more structured way, our Planned Giving Office has suggestions about estate planning, annuities, and even gifts of stock that avoid capital gains taxes.

Maybe you have land that you would like to preserve as a lasting habitat for wildlife. Our Wildlife Land Trust can help you. Perhaps the land you want to share is a backyard—that's enough. Our Urban Wildlife Sanctuary Program will show you how to create a habitat for your wild neighbors.

So you see, it's easy to help animals. And The HSUS is here to help.

THE HUMANE SOCIETY
OF THE UNITED STATES.

2100 L Street NW • Washington, DC 20037 • 202-452-1100
www.hsus.org

Acknowledgements

I would like to thank all the staff members at colleges and universities across the country that helped with this book.

This book is dedicated to Tom Harvey, the teacher I will never forget.

Trademark Statement

Table of Contents

Chapter 3: Designing Your Course   63

Chapter 4: Choosing the Best Textbooks 73

Chapter 5: High-Tech Learning 77

Chapter 8: The Art of Lecturing   129

Chapter 9: Great Debates   143

Chapter 10: Getting to Know Your Students   153

Chapter 14: Problem Students   215

Chapter 15: Plagiarism and Cheating   223

Chapter 16: The Politics
of Being a College Teacher   235

Introduction

Imagine you have just arrived for your first class. The feeling you get can be compared to sitting at the crest of a roller coaster, waiting to take the first plunge. Your stomach fills with butterflies as you realize there is no turning back. You know the ride will be fun, but you have concerns about getting through it.

Maybe you imagine lecturing before a room filled with attentive students who are on fire to learn about the topic you are teaching. Some of the students have already studied your topic and are eager to learn more. Your classroom is a sea of smiling faces focused on everything you say. Your witty opening comments are answered with laughter. Everyone is excited about the work you have outlined for the coming semester.

What if you make your entrance and realize most of the students barely notice you entered the room? They are talking amongst themselves, checking e-mail, or downloading music to their MP3 players. When you finally get their attention, rows of blank, disinterested faces stare back at you. Maybe the lecture hall is so large that you cannot see the students sitting in the last row.

Try not to dwell on everything that might or might not happen; it will only detract from your focus and create unnecessary fear. Relax. This book will cover ways to plant a firm foundation on your first day and carry it through your entire first year. You will learn concrete ways to design a syllabus, introduce yourself to the class, and create interactive lessons with your students. On the other hand, this information should serve as a guideline, not a script. It is always up to you to adapt the basic techniques you learn to best suit the needs of your students. All of this takes time.

Keeping that in mind, know that all of your goals will not be met in one day or even one year. Like every profession, there is an art to teaching. Your natural teaching skills are polished only by experience, mainly by trial and error. Think about your own academic experience. You had to learn how to study and manage your course load. In time, you discovered what worked and what did not. If you prepared for a test at the last minute and gave it little effort, the results were probably not so good. When you put in the effort needed to prepare, things run more smoothly. You can expect to put in some extra hours as a new college teacher. Do not cut corners in building your course or relationships with your students.

Many of your teaching "mistakes" will not even register. You will be teaching some day and suddenly realize you presented something out of order or left a topic out completely. Mistakes will happen, but being well-prepared for every class will help you eliminate them, or figure out your next move. You simply adjust, cover up the mistake, and move on. It is somewhat similar to a professional theater production. As you sit in the audience, everything appears flawless. Most often, only the performers know if they flubbed a line or their pirouette was a little shaky — and no performance is ever perfect. Performers use their confidence and command of the stage to smooth over the rough parts and go on with the show. As a teacher, you are bound to make errors. You, too, will learn to cover your mistakes. In no way should this be interpreted as saying it is acceptable to ever — even once — be sloppy or unprepared. That will simply not fly with your students or your supervisors. When you make a mistake, correct it and learn from it. There is no need to beat yourself up over the occasional mistake.

Be kind to yourself. Your first year of teaching is not a time to become frustrated by a set of unrealistic expectations. Do not expect to be nominated for the college President and Provost Award for Teaching Excellence after one semester. The rewards and recognition will come. Imagine the first time a student approaches you in the hallway and tells you how much he or she enjoys your class. It might not be an impressive gold plaque to hang on the wall, but for a first-year teacher it is a great compliment.

During your first year, especially before your first class, it is normal to be apprehensive as you wade into uncharted waters. This book can help serve as your lifejacket. There are many techniques successful college teachers use to organize their courses and inspire their students. You can learn some of them right here.

Who Can Use This Book

If you are a recent graduate and new to the field of teaching you will need to establish authority and be a leader for students that might not be much younger than yourself. While experience often makes for the best teacher, the energy and enthusiasm of youth should not be dismissed. Use youth to your advantage. One of the hallmarks of a successful teacher is being able to relate to students. You will understand the issues in your younger students' lives better than many of your 55-year-old colleagues because you are closer in age.

Maybe only a few months have passed since you yourself were a student. Consider that an advantage. You have a fresh uderstanding of what makes a good professor. Using your experiences, you can mimic some of your favorite teachers' techniques in your class. Blend your knowledge and experience with the advice in this book and you will be prepared for a rewarding first year of teaching college.

Those who are not recent graduates but are entering the field of teaching for the first time also have certain advantages. Life experiences both in and outside of work will make it easier for an instructor to illustrate how lessons relate to students' future careers. Just as their younger colleagues might be able to connect easier with younger students, older instructors might be more talented at relating to adult learners — a growing population in higher learning institutions.

The task before you is not an easy one. As a new teacher, you might face the added challenge of taking on the least desirable courses and sections.

You might find yourself teaching evenings or early Saturdays. Evening and weekend classes can include many adult learners who have not been in a classroom setting in years or even decades.

Within this book you will find ways to help you measure the knowledge level of your students. These techniques will provide a roadmap for determining the level of complexity and depth you can introduce to your students. Once you know your students' level of knowledge, you can smoothly make modifications to your lesson plans.

No matter what type of student you are teaching, this book will help you effectively organize your courses. The advice can be applied to every kind of faculty — those seeking tenure, adjunct professors, and assistant teachers in graduate programs. All of these positions require the same basic elements: Designing lesson plans, passing your knowledge on to students, adjusting to student-learning styles, and grading student work.

Many of the things you know about teaching are the direct result of what you were taught in college. What about the things you were not taught? Some of these lessons are the most important. Never underestimate the role of office politics in advancing — or squashing — your career. Although you cannot anticipate every political pitfall, this book will cover some of the more common mistakes to avoid.

Maybe you have decided to make a career change and become a college teacher. Perhaps you were previously a college teacher and are now planning to return to the profession. You might only be exploring the possibility of teaching college at this point. Either way, you know being a teacher is one of the most challenging and rewading careers you can ever have. You see it as an exciting opportunity limited only by your imagination and desire to succeed. As you begin this new adventure, approach it with passion, determination, and a sense of humor, because your first lesson is about to begin.

Chapter 1

Getting Started

The first step on the journey to a successful first year is, of course, getting your first job. All new teachers must decide the kind of teaching position to apply for and accept. Your first job will set the course of your pay level and opportunities for advancement. It also sets the tone for your entire teaching career, so choose it carefully. In the following sections you will find some tips for landing your first teaching job, and for deciding on which ones to apply for. The information can also serve as a refresher course if you ever decide to seek a new teaching position. To get started, let us look at the different kind of teaching positions offered at colleges and universities.

Types of Teaching Positions

Faculty

Full-time faculty members draw the highest pay, and they conduct more research than their part-time colleagues. They are assigned to departments or divisions according to subject, and typically teach several different courses. Some faculty members teach only undergraduate or only graduate students, while others teach both. As a faculty member, you can immerse yourself in research and spend countless hours collecting and analyzing data. You will enjoy the prestige of having your research published and seeing your name in journals, books, or electronic media. If you are a full-time faculty member, researching, writing, and publishing your work is not only expected, it is often required. There is variation regarding how much time faculty devote to teaching, conducting research, and other duties. It depends on the expectations and requirements of the institution where you are teaching. Make sure to organize your time for everything you will be expected to do as a new college teacher.

TEACHER'S
TIP:

Faculty positions offer the best job security.

Your work will extend well beyond your classroom and office hours. You must also keep up-to-date in your area of study. This means reading current publications, meeting with colleagues, and participating in conferences. Faculty members sometimes serve on college or department committees, helping to shape departmental issues, academics, budgets, purchasing, and hiring new employees. In addition to all of these college-related activities, expect to do some faculty work with civic groups, as well.

The above tasks are more than enough to fill the day, yet we still have not covered everything that might be part of your schedule. Your course load might be heavier or lighter depending on where you teach. Surprisingly, the prestigious colleges might not be the ones to require more work. Consider these guidelines offered by the U.S. Department of Labor:

2

- Universities require faculty to spend much of their time doing research. At four year-colleges, it is slightly less. Faculty at two-year colleges might not be required to do any research.

- Two-year colleges have a heavier teaching load than four-year colleges.

- Professors have reached the pinnacle of their fields. At any institution, they are allowed to spend the most time doing research.

- Faculty can also work in career-related training programs. These programs cater to working adults. Many of the courses are offered online. Most of the instructors in career-related training programs work part-time. They are the least likely to do research or have administrative responsibilities.

Adjunct

Adjunct teachers are the little guys who do most of the grunt work. The pay and upward mobility is somewhat limited. Before running in the other direction, at least entertain the possibility that being a part-time teacher might be right for you. People sometimes fall into part-time teaching because of tight college budgets, not necessarily because of their potential as a teacher. Being a part-time college teacher might be a good fit if you have connected with a nearby college, but no full-time positions are currently available. Maybe you are seeking a little extra income, but you do not want to give up your day job. You might even be wondering if college teaching is the best career for you and if you really have what it takes. You need a crash course in the basics. You will get it right here.

Many adjunct faculty members have other jobs or commitments that do not allow them to teach full-time, or they might teach at several different institutions because they were unable to acquire a full-time position at one college. Jumping from campus to campus is an option if you live in an area with many colleges within driving distance. Be warned that teaching for multiple colleges can be hectic as you try to juggle all of your schedules. You might find yourself speeding down the freeway with minutes to spare as you race to your next class. You will also have to keep track of all the varying policies and procedures for each college.

To truly succeed, you will need to learn the culture and the politics of each college. It is easy to feel disconnected when you are not working for an institution full-time. If you want to get more "linked in," consider going through an orientation program for new teachers. You can also talk to students and other teachers about the pros and cons of the campus. You can do this by connecting with students and faculty members at campus meetings, researching college forums online, and simply asking individuals who work at or attend the school. Getting to know everything you can about your college increases your success of fitting in.

TEACHER'S TIP:

Teaching college part-time allows you to keep your current career.

Starting off as an adjunct professor offers advantages such as flexibility and the option of keeping your full-time career. The two jobs can complement each other. You might even decide you love teaching so much that you want to do it full time.

Still not sure if part-time teaching is right for you? Here are a few advantages and disadvantages to consider.

Advantages

- Sharing your passion and expertise about your favorite topics

- Additional income

- Focusing on teaching without worrying about serving on various college committees

- Applying only for the classes you want to teach

- Flexible hours

- The ability to have other commitments

Disadvantages

- No long-term job security

- A lack of opportunities for advancement

- No office to meet with students, make phone calls, or do work on campus

- No health insurance, life insurance, or other benefits

- No full-time salary

- Less prestige than being full-time faculty member

- You will still be required to have a master's degree

If you are starting off as an adjunct professor, consider your long-term goals. Adjunct teaching is a good option if you have no aspirations of being a faculty member. Some experts say that typecasting can make it politically difficult to make the switch from part- to full-time. Be aware that there could be a stigma attached to being a part-time teacher. It is possible, but not very easy or likely, to become a faculty member if you start out teaching part-time. Sadly, a college is less likely to move you into a higher-paying position if they can get the same amount of work out of you for a fraction of the cost.

Do not write off becoming a part-time college teacher. Consider if it is right for you, as you can gain much experience from this opportunity.

Assistant teachers

Graduate teaching assistants work as part-time instructors at the college where they are working toward their degree. To get this job, you must be in a graduate degree program. You might also be required to take additional classes or receive additional training before teaching at the college.

Teaching assistants perform a wide range of duties, including preparing lectures and exams, issuing student grades, conducting research, attending faculty and committee meetings, curriculum development, grading papers, monitoring students taking exams, holding office hours or tutoring sessions for students, conducting labs, and giving quizzes.

Do not be afraid to ask for help during your first year of teaching. A mentor can share knowledge that could take years for you learn.

Teaching assistants might also teach classes under the guidance of a mentor. Depending on the needs of the professor, a teaching assistant can be partly or fully responsible for a class. This experience offers a great opportunity to plan and design a course before stepping into a full-time position. On the other hand, it can be very challenging to coordinate your teaching responsibilities while pursuing a graduate degree. Many master's degree programs require you to maintain at least a "B" average. If you miss the mark, you might be asked to leave the program. Make an honest assessment of your abilities and then decide whether being a teaching assistant is the right route to take. If you are not certain, ask one of your trusted college teachers to give you an opinion.

If you become an assistant college teacher, you must have excellent communication with your professor to make sure you understand all of your duties. Your college might also have handbooks or other resources for teaching assistants that will help you understand the expectations and requirements.

One of the biggest benefits of being an assistant teacher is having the opportunity to be mentored by an experienced faculty member. If you are moving into your first teaching job without this training, you might want to ask if a mentor can be assigned to you.

Learning to Teach

Your first year in the college classroom will be a time of teaching and learning more about how to teach. If possible, try to find someone on campus who is willing to serve as your mentor. This person is an experienced teacher who will help guide you through your first year of college. In short, a mentor can help you learn how to be a good college teacher much faster than you can on your own. You will meet with your mentor frequently and they will give you feedback on your performance. They might also watch your lectures and offer some constructive criticism.

TEACHER'S **TIP:**

If possible, get a mentor in your first year of teaching college.

If a formal mentoring program is not available and you are unable to find an informal mentor, ask colleagues and administrators in your department if they know of any good books about teaching. You can also find out if there are any seminars on campus or in the community that can help you learn more about teaching.

The Job Description

Do you have what it takes to be a college teacher? Are you up to the task of shaping the next generation of professionals and future leaders in our nation? Would you like be an expert in your field of study, conducting research or experiments, and publishing your findings in articles or books? If this is appealing, you might have what it takes to consider being a university or college teacher.

The demands of teaching are high. You will be expected to meet demanding performance standards in a variety of areas. The following job description is designed to give you a feel for some of the requirements of being a college teacher. You can find some sample job postings in the appendix of this book. No matter your setting, this description represents the basic duties you will perform as a college teacher.

Job description

You will share your knowledge with students and inspire them to use creative and critical skills as they learn. You will design courses and exams, assess student-learning styles, and grade student work. Advising students and preparing lectures is also part of the job duty. Other duties might include attending department meetings, involvement on faculty committees, conducting workshops, and networking with your peers on campus and at other institutions. The number of students you instruct can vary.

You might lecture hundreds of students in a large auditorium, oversee student laboratory work, or teach small seminars.

Positions as a full-time faculty member generally require a master's degree or a Ph.D., and sometimes specialized expertise in a certain discipline, especially at large or prestigious colleges and universities. Expect your workload to extend well beyond the classroom. You will be expected to keep up on the latest trends in your field, discuss them with colleagues, and meet with community members and business leaders. Another important duty is to keep in touch with the business community and ensure students are being taught the skills that businesses are seeking.

Computer technology adds another layer of duties for you. You will need to be computer and Internet savvy to communicate with your students. Most likely, you will have your own Web site or a chat board where you can post course assignments, notes, and other information. You might teach distance learning courses, which rely solely on the Internet to teach students off-campus or in remote classrooms. These classes are particularly popular with students who work because they are not tied to a specific class time and can complete the work when it is convenient for them. The skills needed for teaching online classes include taking existing courses and converting them into an online version. It is a task that can be very time-consuming, depending on the course. Some colleges might require you to have some online teaching experience.

Other desired qualifications

- A love of education and working with students
- Communication skills
- Creativity
- An ability to inspire and relate to students

- Respect for student diversity and different learning styles

- Encouraging of cooperation, mutual respect, and support among staffers and students

Education requirements

A minimum of a master's degree will be required for virtually all college teaching positions. A Ph.D. is preferred. The only exception might be teaching at vocational or technical colleges. These colleges might consider experience and expertise as being more important than holding an advanced degree.

Many colleges will require teachers to have a master's degree in the field that they are teaching. However, a Ph.D. is preferred.

The education requirements are highest for teachers at research-based universities, where a Ph.D. is considered the standard. Candidates with master's degrees or those who are doctoral candidates might be considered for some disciplines or for adjunct positions.

Generally, it takes a bachelor's degree and six additional years of full-time study to earn a doctorate degree. Doctoral candidates also write a dissertation that involves extensive research in their chosen area of study. The dissertation involves one to two years of full-time work, usually under the supervision of one or more faculty advisors. Career and technical education teachers can usually get a teaching job with a bachelor's degree and at least three years of work experience in the discipline they will be teaching.

You might be required to take courses to update your skills or obtain certifications in your field. Some career and technical schools now include academic courses that provide students with more depth and detail to aid them in landing their first job. Teachers in these programs often help students move from school to work, setting up internship programs and developing relationships with prospective employers.

Salary

The size of your salary hinges on the size of the institution, where the school is located, and whether you are a full- or part-time teacher. Part-time instructors often paid hourly or per credit hour, so the number of courses they take on affects their earnings. Full-time instructors are likely salaried and, in addition to their pay, typically earn benefits that adjunct instructors do not receive, such as health and life insurance. Teachers at two-year institutions generally earn less than those at four-year schools. A teacher's degree can affect pay; individuals with Ph.D.s generally earn at least $6,000 more per year than those with master's degrees. Earnings also vary by field.

Working environment

Most of your colleagues will be passionate about their subjects, so you will have the opportunity to work with people who love their jobs. This can in turn inspire you to do a better job. Whether it is competitive spirit, collegiate support, or simple inspiration, the effects of surrounding yourself with talented coworkers will serve to drive your own aspirations.

Most full-time teaching jobs are lauded for their great hours and generous chunks of time off. You will most likely be scheduled to work only about nine months of the year due to holidays, student breaks, and time off. If you are working part time in your first year, then obviously you will be teaching fewer classes. Even so, you might be surprised at just how many hours it will take you to do all of your work. Whether you teach full- or part-time, teaching college is not a 9-to-5 job. You might teach classes at night or on the weekends. Expect to teach a night or weekend class if you work at an institution with large numbers of students with families or full-time jobs. This is highly likely at community colleges and "commuter colleges" with high numbers of adult students who work or have other responsibilities. You will probably teach classes for 12 to 16 hours a week, and have hours set aside for office time to meet with students. You get to decide how long it takes to prepare for your courses, grade student work, and conduct research.

As a new teacher, your actual time off might be precious little. You can expect to work more than 40 hours a week. It might even be 80 hours, as some new teachers spend their time off working as well. Use caution in this area. Everyone needs time to relax and recharge.

Part of the problem for a new teacher is the learning curve. You cannot expect to be as fast as a veteran teacher in class preparation, grading, and advising students. Also consider the difficulty level of your classes. You might not be teaching graduate-level classes in your first year. Still, classes for undergraduate majors might be more difficult than classes for non-majors. That means you will need a deeper knowledge of your topic.

Other things, such as research, will also add time to your schedule. Even if formal research is not required in your position, you will want to remain current on what is happening in your field. You will do research through discussions with your colleagues, conferences, and reading written materials and experiments (if this applies to your field). Your college might also have expectations that you will attend conferences and get involved in campus clubs or community groups. All of these factors can add considerable time to your schedule.

Let us take a look at what a typical day might look like for a full-time college teacher.

> 6 a.m. — You will likely be up and getting ready if you have an early class. Now is the time to take a quick look through your e-mails and respond to the most pressing messages. Then get your materials ready for class, and off you go.
>
> 7:30 a.m. to 8:30 a.m. — Arrive at the campus. Allow yourself some time to get your materials organized and answer questions from students who might stop by your office.
>
> 9 a.m. to 4 p.m. — This time can include a variety of classes, office hours, lunch, and meetings with students or faculty members. If you have any downtime, you might be able to grade your students' work.
>
> 4 p.m. to 9 p.m. — Grading assignments and attending workshops or community events.

Most colleges and universities require teachers to work nine months of the year, which allows them time during the summer and school holidays to teach additional courses, do research, travel, or pursue nonacademic interests.

Now you should know for certain if you have the skills and education required to succeed as a first-year teacher. You have passed the criteria test; now for the ultimate test. Answer the question, "Why do I want to be a college teacher?"

Why Do You Want to Teach?

CASE STUDY: WHY I BECAME A TEACHER

Michelle A. Blackley
Adjunct teacher, communications
Buffalo State University and
Genesee Community College

Michelle Blackley landed her first collegiate teaching job on a fluke. She had just returned to her hometown of Buffalo, New York from New York City, where she worked in publishing for approximately five years. Blackley enjoyed her job in the big city, but the quality of life left something to be desired. By returning to Buffalo, she was able to afford larger living accommodations, have a car, and be closer to her family.

Blackley, who has a master's degree in speech communication, spotted an advertisement in a local paper for an assistant professor position. She sent in a letter to see if she was qualified and if the school had any part-time openings. That summer, she taught her first class in media literacy.

"I really went to school to become a teacher," Blackley said. "I always enjoyed being in an academic environment, and I liked being around the students. Things change every semester and it has just seemed to work out really well for me."

But it was not right away that she really loved teaching. It took her a few semesters, she said. Seeing students build confidence throughout the course of her speech and public speaking classes is what is rewarding for Blackley.

"I still remember what it is like to be a young person," she said. "When I see them getting stressed out at mid-semester over everything they have to do, I understand."

There is a lot to do in Buffalo, Blackley said. Not only does she have a better quality of life than in New York, but she gets to enjoy teaching.

Before becoming a college teacher, consider your reason for wanting to do this job. Is it shaping the future lives of your students? Making a difference in the world? Is it giving dynamic lectures worthy of a standing ovation? Maybe the perks are your main draw: a good paycheck, summers off, and the prestige of being an expert in your field. Is teaching a long-time passion, or is it a bridge to fill a gap between careers? If it is the latter, the demands of being a college professor will probably leave you stressed out and frustrated, even if you do it part-time.

Ultimately, you will get the most satisfaction from teaching if you want to do it for the right reasons. Earning good money and having a flexible schedule are simply the benefits of being a teacher. They will not be enough to hold you in a demanding career you do not truly love.

Your enthusiasm for teaching will go a long way in determining how effective you will be. Whether you are passionate about mathematics or philosophy, your love of your topic will spill over to your students. Perhaps most importantly, teachers care about their students. They enjoy watching students expand their knowledge and succeed in the classroom. At some point you might have said, "I want to inspire people the way my favorite teacher inspired me."

Write down the top three reasons why you want to be a college teacher and be honest. This will be your mission statement. Hopefully, what you wrote down emphasizes your desire to shape young adult minds and teach them to become avid learners.

Now that you have your mission statement, vow to place it in a spot where you can see it every day. On days you ask aloud, "Why did I ever decide to become a college teacher?" you will have your answer. In time, your mission statement might be modified. Modifying your mission statement allows you to re-examine your goals and motivations and adapt your teaching style accordingly. Also, objectives, such as whether to pursue tenure or not, might shift in the future.

It also helps to understand your strengths and views about teaching. Do you enjoy dynamic lectures, or are you more comfortable with discussion groups? Which style best fits the topic you are teaching? There is never a perfect answer to any of these questions. Every classroom is different and each group of students you encounter will be different. Teaching is an ongoing learning process.

Do not assume you must always imitate your favorite teachers. Draw on your own strengths, but be open to changing or expanding your teaching techniques.

Outlook for College Teaching

Before the economy officially soured in late 2008, the job outlook for college teachers was stronger than for most other professions. The U.S. Bureau of Labor Statistics projected that between 2006 and 2016, the number of postsecondary teaching positions would grow by about 23 percent, or 382,000 jobs. These studies showed that college teaching jobs had a faster average growth than many other occupations. However, the economic downturn left no profession unscathed. Colleges saw funding cuts, salary freezes, and layoffs. These factors varied by the college and the general economy of the region where it is located, meaning that some areas of the country fared better than others during economic slowdowns.

TEACHER'S TIP:

Teaching is projected to be a high-growth, high-demand career for many years.

Starting in the early 2000s, the opportunity for tenured faculty positions began declining, according to the U.S. Department of Education. One reason for the trend can be traced to a reduction in state and federal funding for higher-learning institutions, according to the Education Resources Information Center Clearinghouse on Higher Education. This, in turn, resulted in cost-cutting measures.

As with any teaching job, some subjects will be in higher demand. This will also vary depending on the university or college. The cost-cutting measures colleges have already put in place, coupled with a recession, can make it fiercely competitive to land a full-time teaching position. For the most part, education careers have been insulated from the impact of the recession.

On the plus side, many laid-off employees are working people going back to college to finish their degrees or get additional training. Financial analysts cite education as one of the most stable industries. Part of the reason is a wave of retirements that is expected to create many new openings for college teachers. Adults looking to update their job skills will also add to new job openings for postsecondary teachers, especially at colleges that cater to working adults.

The job forecast also calls for an increase in careers requiring technical skills, which will create more jobs for teachers in vocational programs. Community colleges and vocational schools are among the fastest growing programs. According to labor studies, careers related to health care, business, construction, and technology are also growing.

There will be plenty of teaching opportunities out there, especially in these high-demand areas. So how you can find these jobs?

Where and how to find teaching jobs

If you are searching for a college teaching job, there are plenty of Web sites that list openings. Here are a few:

> Higher Ed Jobs
> **www.higheredjobs.com/**
> Daily updated list of faculty and administrative posts at colleges and universities in the United States and Canada

> CollegeGrad.com
> **www.collegegrad.com/college/college-teaching-jobs.shtml**
> A site that lists entry-level positions for recent graduates

Educationamerica.net

www.educationamerica.net/

Includes overseas teaching positions

Academic 360

www.academic360.com/

Lists available faculty positions by discipline

AcademicKeys.com

www.academickeys.com/

Has a job search function and lists of "Who's Who" in various disciplines and academic resources

While the Web is a helpful tool in finding a job, do not let it limit your search. It is often said that most jobs are found through networking.

Reach out to family members, neighbors, friends, coworkers, former employers, and former college teachers to see if they can offer you any insight into some of the institutions where you plan to apply. Networking often has a positive domino effect, meaning that a person you talk to might know of someone else who has a job lead, and so on. If you are looking for an adjunct position, consider applying at several nearby colleges. There is a good chance that you will find an opening as the turnover rate is fairly high for part-time positions.

Professional societies related to specific fields often have information on available teaching positions. The Chronicle of Higher Education lists faculty opportunities on its Web site. This publication is likely available at your local library. Additional teaching positions can be found by searching state or national career development programs.

Chapter 2

Landing Your First Job

There are many decisions that go into finding a first job, especially your first job as a college professor. For instance, you may have a certain college that you are particularly fond of, maybe because of location or its athletic department, or you may choose to go somewhere that has a strong department for the subject you will be teaching. Or, you may not want to move from where you are currently living, so finding a college or university in your state is a priority. Regardless of the reasons that drive where you take your first job, you need to consider things like your location, your previous work experience, and your desired salary.

Deciding Where to Live

As a new teacher, be prepared to move to where the jobs are available. But if you have a choice, here are some factors to take into consideration:

- The weather: If you love warm climates, a job in Minnesota would not be right for you. A city dweller might be unhappy living in Podunk, Pennsylvania, just as a country dweller would feel overwhelmed in New York City.

TEACHER'S TIP:

If a move is required for your first teaching job, you should consider the cost of housing, local and state taxes, the quality of schools for your children — even the climate.

- "Real pay": This means taking into account the local cost of living — housing, local and state taxes, and the quality of schools for your children, to name a few. Be careful when researching cities. The cost of living can be much higher in the nice communities surrounding major metropolitan areas.

- Commute: Depending on the size of the city and its traffic system, you can face a lengthy commute even if you live just a few miles away. Daily traffic jams drain your time; time you could have spent designing your course instead of sitting in traffic. However, if you do not anticipate needing your car too much during the day, public transportation might be an option. A speedy subway system can save you time, although standing on a corner waiting for a bus might take longer than sitting in traffic. You may also live far away from the campus, which means you automatically have a long drive to and from work every day, in addition to any traffic or weather conditions that could make your commute even longer.

Developing a Résumé and References

A résumé is often the first introduction you will make to an institution, so it needs to create a favorable impression of you. Consider paying a professional to write your résumé and cover letter. If you decide to do it yourself, use professional and easy-to-read fonts, such as Times New Roman. Use heavy, white paper that is free of smudges and wear.

Writing your cover letter

The purpose of your cover letter is to get you an interview and, ultimately, a job. Your cover letter should entice the reader to want to continue on to the résumé. First, let us start with the basics. Always address your letter to a person, not just a department at a college. Call the college and make sure you have the correct name and title (and spelling) of the person who will receive your application. Cover letters, like résumés, should be brief and professional in tone. This suggests you can quickly and succinctly organize your thoughts — an important trait for a teacher. Resist the urge to be clever or make puns. Instead, use professional, college-level language. After you write your cover letter, rewrite it. Tighten up the wording and make sure it sings. You want to sell yourself, but be realistic in what you are promising. Do not declare things you have not really accomplished or things you doubt you might be able to fulfill.

Writing your résumé

Writing a résumé can be a daunting task, especially for a new teacher. Many teachers straight from college have little or no work experience. Their educational backgrounds will provide most of the content for their résumés. If you are making a career switch, you will likely have to overhaul your current résumé. When reworking your résumé, think of how your work experience has provided you with skills that relate to being a good teacher. This can include being organized, showing leadership, public speaking, managing others, and working as a part of a team.

As a general rule, your résumé should be kept to one page. You want to quickly capture the attention of the person screening résumés. Do not stretch the facts, yet do not be afraid to highlight your achievements. A great résumé is credible, but also makes you stand out from the sea of other candidates.

Here are the basic sections your résumé should have:

Contact information

This includes your name, address, phone numbers, and e-mail address. If you are still on campus when you apply, list your current and permanent addresses. It is fine to specify how long you will remain on campus and where you can be reached after the semester.

Objective

Include the subjects you are qualified to teach. A statement about how you plan to make teaching college your career is also good to include. If you have an interest in supervising any extra-curricular activities it is fine to include that, as well. Keep in mind that it is best to leave this portion of your résumé brief. Use your cover letter to expand on your qualifications and goals.

Education

This section should come directly after the objective, unless you have professional experience related to teaching. For example, you might have worked in a pre-school center over the summer. If you have a master's degree, that should be listed first. Then list your bachelor's degree. List your grade-point average if it is higher than 3.0.

Experience or "Additional Experience"

Any work experience that involves teaching or tutoring — even if it was a volunteering position — should be listed under experience. Consider including experience that shows you have an interest in teaching and would make an excellent teacher. Teacher-related experience should take precedence over positions that were paid. If you worked to help pay your way through school, that shows a certain degree of responsibility. It is worth mentioning, but is not worth a lot of detail on your résumé. Whatever you mention, try to legitimately make it relate to teaching.

Professional associations and other groups

List college clubs or community groups if they relate to teaching or allowed you to develop skills that would be relevant to teaching. This is even better if you have received any awards or recognitions from these groups. Always focus the information you give on how your experiences will make you a great educator. Leave off high school clubs and awards unless you are a recent college graduate and the achievement was extraordinary. Personal hobbies and interests are best left off your résumé. If you like to play golf or water ski, bring it up in the interview *if you are asked* about the interests you have outside of teaching. This shows you are well-rounded and less likely to burn out from doing nothing but teaching or thinking about teaching 24-7.

Web sites and blogs

If you write an education-related blog or Web site, it is fine to list it. Do not offer links to personal social media pages, especially if you have posted pictures of a crazy party you attended while vacationing in Cancun. Social media shenanigans are fun for friends, but it could raise questions about your professionalism or put you out of the running for a job. Always use good judgment in what you post or reveal online.

When designing a résumé, make it specific to the college where you are sending your application. Interview committees will often go through a checklist to decide whom to bring in for an interview. If you inadvertently leave something off, you might eliminate yourself. How can you know what an institution is seeking? Carefully read the job description. Incorporate some of the key words they use into your résumé. Many organizations today scan résumés into computers that use software programs to hunt for key words. As always, follow the instructions of the institution when applying. Here are some basic tips for building a résumé:

- Screening committees expect neatness. Typos and spelling and grammatical errors could take you out of the running for a position.

- If an application form is available, submit it along with your résumé.

- Include curriculum vitae, a listing of your professional accomplishments. Do not send one in lieu of a résumé, unless it is requested. Also, take time to look over your curriculum vitae before an interview. This will provide a road map of your experience and can help you discuss your qualifications more easily.

- Use your cover letter to highlight how your experience will help the college.

- Send only the information requested. Do not send research reports, articles, course outlines, or writing samples unless they are requested.

If you get an interview, research the institution. Learn about its enrollment, administration, and its history. Most interviewers will ask questions that gauge whether you have done your homework. If you do not seem to know the basics, you might be passed over.

Now that you know how to prepare for an interview, you need to understand what to expect during an interview for a college teaching position. Knowing what to expect and how to answer the questions will greatly increase your chances of being hired.

References

Choose your references carefully. You want people who are going to return the phone calls from the colleges where you are applying. Selecting people who fail to respond will reflect poorly on you. The person doing the calling might even view it as a bad reference or poor judgment on your part. Of course, returning the call is not all that matters. You only want references that are going to give an excellent review of your performance, personality, and work habits. Never use someone as a reference unless you have received his or her permission. Ask if they would feel comfortable giving you a great recommendation. If they are enthusiastic about helping you, then you have found an ideal reference.

TEACHER'S **TIP:**

Be picky when choosing work references. Make sure they will return reference requests and will give you a glowing review.

Request that a teacher or former employer put their recommendation in writing so you can place a copy with your résumé. This makes the reference readily available, and a potential employer only has to call to verify who sent it. If a professor or a former employer refuses to give a written reference, you might want to ask yourself if that person or employer will truly make a good reference. For the same reason, always ask before using anyone as a reference. If an employer calls and catches them off-guard, it could create a bad impression. If a few months pass before you accept an offer, call your references and remind them you are still looking and they might be receiving a telephone call. The same applies if you ever change jobs in the future. Do not list someone you used as a reference five years ago without first calling them.

The people you use as references can be former teachers, employers, or people from organizations where you have volunteered. Round up several people, and have a couple of backups if possible. Five strong references should be enough. If you can get more references, add them to your list as alternates. Unless it is specifically spelled out, you will probably not be asked to provide more than three references. If you have not spoken to your references in a while, call and remind them that you are using them as a reference. The last thing you want an interviewer to hear from one of your references is, "Oh, Bill! I hope he is doing well. I have not heard from him in months." This might raise questions about your judgment and your communication skills. When it is something as serious as landing a new job, you want to make sure every detail is covered. This includes having good references, and making sure they are aware when someone might be calling them.

What to Expect During an Interview

Interviewing for a postsecondary-level teaching position can make you feel overly scrutinized. Instead of panicking, approach the interview as though you would be doing the institution a favor by allowing them to hire you. Do not come across arrogant, but convince them you are the best candidate for the position and "sell" yourself to the interviewer. Research what qualities the college wants in an ideal candidate and use that information to illustrate how your skills make you the one for the job. Knowing this information allows you to structure your answers to fit their needs.

You will face some tricky questions. Some of these questions are designed to see how quickly you respond and if your answers match the details of your résumé. Although you cannot predict every question that will be asked, questions about potential red flag issues, such as gaps in college enrollment or employment history, are bound to come up. Anticipate these questions and rehearse your answers in advance so that you do not fumble over your answers.

Career consultants say it is best to answer every question in two minutes or less. Make sure you are answering the specific question you are asked. It is fine to ask the interviewer for clarification about a question if you did not understand it. When you answer, avoid the temptation to bombard the interviewer with anecdotes. Venturing away from the topic with personal information could lead to a foot-in-mouth situation, or can cause you to ramble. Some interviewers will sit silently after you answer a question, just to see if you start to ramble. Often, interviewers will give you the silent treatment after asking a sensitive question, often about your race, sexual orientation, history of drug or alcohol addiction, and the sort. By law, potential employers are not permitted to ask these types of questions on a first interview, but that does not mean that some interviewers will not try just to see if they can get you to respond. If the silence seems to drag on forever, you might ask the interviewer if they need any additional information. Be sure to sound helpful, not confrontational.

TEACHER'S TIP:

Answer interview questions succinctly and honestly. Do not ramble, and try to keep your answers to two minutes or less.

You might be asked to demonstrate a lesson in front of a panel of interviewers. Be prepared to demonstrate that you have the tools and the skills it takes to be a good teacher. If you are asked to conduct a teaching demonstration, make sure you understand what the interviewer is seeking. Adhere to the time frame you are given and use the same techniques you would use in your classroom.

To sharpen your interviewing skills, ask a couple of family members or friends if they will help you conduct a mock job interview. An even better option is to contact a free career counseling service in your town. Your local labor department probably has a host of job search workshops available at no cost. Churches and civic groups are another good resource. If possible, do mock interviews with complete strangers, as you might be too comfortable with friends or family members. Selling your abilities to a total stranger will help soothe any nervousness and focus your responses. The "professionals" will be able to honestly critique your performance. They are more likely to tell you that you are mumbling your responses or looking at the floor too much.

Interview Questions

Here are some common interview questions, followed by guidelines on how to answer them. It is important to think about the types of things you may be asked in an interview before you are sitting in the conference room with your potential employer so that you can be prepared for anything that is thrown your way.

What are some of your weaknesses?

Try to present a weakness as a problem you are conquering, or mention a past weakness you have since learned to overcome. For example, "A weakness I once had was time management. During college, I withdrew from two classes. I realized it was due to my lack of time management skills. After finding new ways to manage my time, I was able to make up the classes, raise my grade point average, and complete my degree on time."

What are some of your strengths?

This should be your favorite question. Using your own strengths, gear your answer toward revealing yourself to be the ideal candidate you know the college is looking for.

What did you like least about college?

Do not complain about the workload, your professors, or college policies. You could raise doubts about whether you will complain about the institution where you are applying. Try to pick something incidental. "It was always a challenge to find parking, so I made sure I allowed myself extra time to get to my classes on time." Once again, you have illustrated how you overcame a problem.

Why do you like teaching?

In Chapter One you were asked to write down the top reasons you want to teach. Draw upon them to answer this question. However, if you listed extended time off and other perks, this is absolutely not the time to bring them up. Emphasize your interest in helping students succeed. Show how your passion for teaching and your skills will add value to the institution.

What courses would you really like to teach and how would you teach them?

Research what you believe the college needs. It is also good to have an innovative example that you think the college might like.

What is your ideal teaching position?

Your answer should be nothing less than the exact position you are applying for.

Do you have the stamina for the workload you will be given?

Offer an example of your stamina: "I am certain I can handle the responsibility based on my ability to earn my master's degree with honors while working two part-time jobs."

Are you interested in serving in any non-academic activities?

This usually pertains to smaller colleges. You might be expected to be an advisor for student organizations or other groups at the college. If you have a burning desire to be an assistant football coach or an advisor for the college newspaper (and you are qualified to do either), you just boosted your chances of getting hired.

Are you looking to stay here long term?

This is a variation on the question "Where do you see yourself in five years?" You want to reassure the interviewer that you will be there for the long run. Do not give the impression that you will work at the institution a year or two, and then move on to a larger college. "I am definitely ready to make a long-term commitment to this college. Your requirements and my qualifications are an excellent match, and I am certain that by doing an exemplary job, opportunities for advancement will follow."

Be prepared to answer questions about your spouse and family, especially if the job involves relocating. But, be aware of what questions your interviewers are allowed to ask you, and which ones they are not allowed to ask you. Questions considered off-limits are about age, ethnicity, and religious preference. It is best to consider the context in which the question is being asked. For example, an employer might ask about children because they are wondering about the logistics of your relocation. On the other hand, they might be concerned that you will be frequently absent when the children are ill. There is nothing wrong with answering the questions — unless you give the "wrong" answer. If you refuse to answer and no malice was intended, you could appear difficult and you could lose out on the job. You might try answering in a way that shows you have experience balancing your career with family time. Another possibility is saying, "Yes, I have children, and they are very excited about moving."

How will you fit in, based on our mission statement?

A mission statement is a written description of the institution's purpose, beliefs, and goals. It also outlines the techniques the institution uses to achieve its goals. This question can also be a reflection of how you will be perceived in the community. Again, base your answer on what you have read in the mission statement.

What kind of research have you done?

Try not to go into great detail. The people interviewing you will likely be long-standing faculty and they probably have not done extensive research in a while.

Those applying for tenured faculty positions at colleges and universities might be asked to demonstrate how their research sheds new light on their topic, how it compares to other scholars in the same field, and whether it can be explained to an average, educated person. Your answer will depend on your field of research. In general, it is good to keep your answer succinct. If the interviewer wants or needs additional information, he or she will ask for it. You might want to have a research paper available as an example of your work.

You can find more examples of common interview questions by conducting an Internet search. A sample of actual college interview questions is included in the appendix of this book.

Interview tips

- Prepare several insightful questions. It shows you have a sincere interest in the job.

- Approach the interviewer or search committee panel in a calm, yet friendly manner.

- Thank the interviewer or search committee for their time and follow up with thank-you cards.

CASE STUDY: HOW TO GET YOUR FIRST TEACHING JOB

Heather Backstrom
First-time adjunct teacher, management & organization behavior & change
University of Redlands in Southern California

When searching for jobs, would-be teachers should know exactly what they want, according to Heather Backstrom, an adjunct teacher at University of Redlands in Southern California.

"In a tight job market – or in any market – knowing what kind of teaching position you want can determine whether or not you will land the job and be successful in it," Backstrom explained. "You should also be very clear about where you want to teach: Is it at the community college level, private, or public institutions? Ask yourself what size classes and which kind of environment you will be the most comfortable with."

In deciding whether to apply at a school, applicants should inquire about what resources are available to the professor as well as to the students. Does the university offer special training or mentoring for first-time teachers?

When searching for a job, Backstrom knew she was not interested in teaching at the community college level, even though she earned part of her education from one, she said. Instead, she was interested in teaching at a private school of a smaller to medium size. In applying to University of Redlands, Backstrom decided to visit the school in person.

"So many positions require candidates to apply online. Either that, or there has to be a connection, or they need to be referred," Backstrom said. "Dropping by takes a little more initiative. It is not something people always think about doing, but I am thankful I did it. I also set my intentions before I went in. I wanted the best possible outcome."

Backstrom researched as much as possible before her interview. "You never know what is going to come up," she said.

She looked up Redlands' history before meeting with staff. Her interviewers asked her what she knew about the school and why she was interested in it. In addition to relaying the information she knew about the school, Backstrom also spoke about her personal connection with the school — her sister is a graduate of their master's degree program in speech pathology, her brother-in-law works at the main campus in the IT department, and Backstrom's grandmother used to clean the university president's house — and of Redlands' reputation of providing high-quality education.

In addition to researching the school, Backstrom said applicants should prepare to show off their teaching skills. "Be prepared to offer a writing sample or to make a presentation. They want to see what your teaching style is, and it would not surprise me if you are asked to do a sample lesson. It can also help to have a writing sample on hand, in case you are asked to submit one. You may also be asked to evaluate a student writing sample during your interview. I was asked to assess and grade a paper, and to write comments that would lead the student toward more academic writing."

Applicants should showcase their real-world experience and how their professional positions relate to teaching, Backstrom said.

"Review the times in your career when you have been teaching. Perhaps you have done workshops and presentations. This can demonstrate your ability to impart information and knowledge in the classroom," she said. "If you have had experiences in working with difficult people, you can relate that to being able to work with a disruptive student."

Questions might crop up about one's teaching philosophy, Backstrom said. She believes what helped her in the interview is that she shared her belief in cooperative learning. She sees her students as equals.

After the interview, Backstrom followed up with a standard thank-you letter. She also dropped a note to the receptionist. Applicants should be sure to thank anyone who helped them along the way.

"Obviously, if you have a genuine love of teaching, that is going to come through. I always knew I loved teaching. I have always enjoyed it and I have been energized doing workshops for human resources. I always sought opportunities to do training, development, and coaching," Backstrom said.

New teachers should view faculty or development meetings as an opportunity to network and expand their knowledge. They should participate in meetings where faculty members discuss classroom standards and university polices. Relationship-building is very valuable, Backstrom said.

Understanding Faculty Contracts and Unions

OK, you have been offered a job. Now what? Do not walk away too satisfied with yourself yet. Always get an employment offer in writing, especially if it will be a while before you sign a contract. With an offer in hand, misunderstandings and "memory lapses" can be avoided.

As with any contract, make sure you thoroughly read and understand it before you sign it. Contract wording can vary and it will be up to you, and possibly your attorney, to determine if there are any problems with the contract.

Pay particular attention to information regarding policies for sabbatical leave, study leave, vacation time, notification of illness, sick time, holidays, mileage and expenses, intellectual copyrights, probationary period, tenure, contract renewals, resignation notices, your tenure status, and research grants.

Your contract might include a statement about "academic freedom." This is an important area, as it will define expectations for the kind of research you are to do. Be sure you understand it. It might include a statement saying you cannot be disciplined or censored for speaking or writing outside of the college. Conversely, there might be potential for discipline if you do or say something that is controversial within the college community. Free speech and free thought are wonderful things, but do not risk offending certain members of the community on or off the campus.

TEACHER'S TIP:

Make sure you thoroughly understand the terms of your teaching contract and get all questions answered before you sign it.

Understanding the terms of your contract is perhaps the most important part. Most college teaching contracts cover nine- or ten-month terms for full-time and part-time faculty. The types of contracts you will most likely encounter include:

- Initial contracts for new, full-time faculty with a monthly salary rate.

- Contracts based on a per-course basis.

- Temporary faculty contracts for graduate and doctoral teaching assistants.

Salary Negotiations

If possible, get a tenure-track job if you have secured a Ph.D. Typically, when a professor has tenure, it means that they have academic freedom and that their contract with a particular university or college cannot be terminated. Having tenure means more job security and perks, such as paid sabbaticals for conducting research, a long-term commitment from an institution, and better pay.

In contrast, the non-tenure-track receives limited contracts without a long-term promise of job security. Expectations for non-tenure staff are lower, too. They do not have to do the same level of research or teaching as their tenured counterparts.

TEACHER'S **TIP:**

Aim as high as possible in terms of prestige and salary. This will set the tone for the rest of your career.

Try to get hired at the best institution, especially if you want to earn a top salary or move to a larger institution. Faculty at four-year colleges and universities will earn more than faculty at two-year colleges. Depending on the institution, salaries for full-time faculty can range from $39,899 to $91,548.

Areas that require a high level of technical skill — such as law, financial management, engineering, business administration, and medicine — are the highest-paying disciplines. Average salaries are usually lower in the humanities fields such as English, history, and philosophy. Higher levels of experience and education open the doors to higher salaries.

Always negotiate for the highest salary you can get. Remember that you might only work for 9 months of the year, but your salary will be spread out over 12 months.

Before negotiating your salary, do a little Internet research on the current range for the position you are applying for. You can look up average salaries based on region, years of experience, and education. Once you are armed with this information, you can use it to justify the salary you want. Approach it with confidence and take the stance that you have nothing to lose.

Future salary increases might be bound by the contract you sign. If the annual increase for everyone under contract is 3 percent, guess what you will be getting? If the college freezes salaries – ditto. Unless you have tenure, which is covered in the next section, you will be bound by the annual percentage increases given by your institution. These percentage increases usually are not that large.

If you have room to negotiate your salary, make sure you can point to concrete examples that demonstrate how you went beyond the basic requirements of the position. If you can do that in your first year of teaching, you definitely deserve a bigger raise. Ask for it.

Parking and Other Benefits

You might not think that parking is significant. But, if you are on a campus where parking is sparse, be sure to ask about places you can park. There are parking fees and then there is reserved parking, while other schools organize lots by color or name, selling decals for certain lots based on faculty position, student credit hours, and other similar things. Reserved parking can cost you nearly $1,000 a year at some schools.

Faculty Unions

You might be asked to join an academic collective bargaining unit, which are also called faculty unions. Collective bargaining units can cover everyone from support staff to faculty on track for tenure. The American Association of University Professors (AAUP), for example, has more than 70 chapters that represent faculty. The AAUP started in the early 1970s to protect professional standards and fight for good faculty salaries. The organization is also concerned with protecting teachers' rights to conduct research without fear of retaliation, providing teachers with protection from being arbitrarily fired, and allowing teachers to participate in making decisions about the institution where they work.

TEACHER'S TIP:

Unions typically require fees, but you will be paid back with greater academic freedom and more job security.

Teachers who belong to a union tend to have more academic freedom. This means they have more liberty to talk about or research controversial topics without fear of retaliation. In fact, one of the prime benefits of belonging to a bargaining unit is that you have greater protection against being released from a position without just cause. There are usually membership dues or annual fees that must be paid before being a member. If you become a member, your individual union will advise you on what they can and cannot help you with. Often, unions will be able to assist you with grievances and any negative reports that come up in relation to your performance. These issues might come from supervisors, students, or parents. Having a union on your side can mean that your side of the story will be taken into consideration. These provisions are secondary to federal labor laws that protect all employees, whether unions represent them or not.

Finally, unions offer a way for teachers to have input on how the college is run. Salaries and schedules go through a formal approval process and generally cannot be arbitrarily changed by college administrators. Union members also have the chance to offer their opinions on these and other issues.

Tenure

Understanding the importance and politics of tenure is critical to your success as a teacher. It will help you establish your goals for the future, as well as help you gain job security. But, what exactly is tenure? It means that the level of your research, teaching, and administrative skills haves been officially recognized. Your job security is placed at a level where you cannot be fired without just cause. Universities are reluctant to give tenure because it allows you to work as long as you choose, whether you are effective or not. The institution might also be reluctant to fire older workers out of fear of an age discrimination lawsuit.

TEACHER'S **TIP:**

Getting tenure is quite an accomplishment and it is not easy to obtain.

Tenure is popular among professors and not so popular with colleges. It is increasingly difficult to achieve tenure. You have probably already guessed that placing people in part-time or adjunct positions saves a college a lot of money.

Other reasons for the decline in tenure include a lack of public trust, new federal policies, costs associated with new technology, competition from for-profit universities, downsizing, and criticisms about tenure. A recent study also cited heavy faculty workloads that can lead to reduced productivity and a surplus of people with Ph.D.s in some fields. Some institutions have policies that allow them to evaluate all faculty members every few years. Those not performing up to par might be "encouraged" to leave, sometimes with payments or by other means.

What about faculty who work under contracts? Some of them complain of reduced job security, a lack of academic creativity or freedom, and a reduction in student-learning. The creative part of having tenure allows you to express your beliefs without fear of retaliation. Without tenure, faculty might be less likely to talk or write about controversial or unpopular views. They could be too worried their contracts will not be renewed.

At schools with low numbers of tenured instructors, student-learning can be impacted because part-time faculty might not have the time to advise or mentor students outside of class. For these reasons, it is questioned whether students receive the attention they need to succeed or move into graduate programs.

Non-tenured staff can be left out of the loop. An "us and them" mentality can result from the higher-paid tenured faculty and the non-tenured faculty. What if you are non-tenure staff and this happens to you? Isolating yourself is never a good approach. Strike up conversations with the tenured staff and look for ways to demonstrate that you are serious about teaching, and that your work adds value to the institution. Some contract workers might not want tenure, however. As previously mentioned, working under contract allows more flexibility for people who have other full-time jobs.

But if tenure is your goal, how exactly can you get it?

Getting tenure

For most college teachers, tenure is the goal. The obvious reason is better pay. There are several steps toward earning tenure. Overall, the process can take about seven years. First, you will need a Ph.D. Some experts say you should not attempt to work full-time and obtain your Ph.D. at the same time because it is too difficult. Imagine teaching full-time while studying for your doctorate and writing for highly-ranked journals and academic publications. If you attempt to do work full-time and earn your doctorate, you will have to complete your doctorate in six years, so it is ready in time for the review committee. Before attempting such a lofty goal, make sure you have the schedule and the stamina to pull it off.

Next, there are several steps in moving up the faculty ranks. First, you might start out as an instructor or assistant professor, then move up to associate professor and, finally, to professor. Those on the tenure-track are usually hired as contract instructors or teaching professors.

To decide if tenure will be granted, institutions review the teaching skills, published papers, and research you have done. If you get a favorable review, tenure is granted. If not, you will probably be asked to leave. As already noted above, having tenure means greater job security. You cannot be fired without due process and just cause.

When it comes to tenure, get it if and while you can. Based on current trends, tenure could become a thing of the past. Changes in funding and retirement laws, along with a reluctance to keep "dead weight," threaten the future of tenure. This does not mean you cannot have a fulfilling and successful career without it. Just be aware that your pay and job security will not be as great.

Chapter 3

Designing Your Course

Congratulations. You have landed your first teaching job and have officially moved from being a student to being a teacher. Now you can begin laying the groundwork for your course. This chapter will help you decide on the pacing, material, and system of delivery for your course in order to best instruct your students.

Rookie teachers too often focus on what they will teach, rather than what students should learn and how they learn. Not only do you want to determine what students learn, you want to equip them to use their knowledge. If you can achieve that, you will empower students to consider different viewpoints. You will help shape their opinions and views of the world. You might be asking how on earth you are going to design a course that accomplishes all of this. Take it one step at a time.

Designing a course starts with one paragraph, called the course introduction. It is simply a statement that explains what the students are going to learn, and what they can do with their knowledge. This paragraph can be displayed in many areas, such as in course description booklets, on your syllabus, and on the class Web site. Keep your course introduction simple to start. You can always revise it and add more information later on.

To make this task a little easier, ask the following questions about your course:

- What is my course about?

- What topics do I enjoy and which ones are most important?

- What should my students know, and what new skills will they have after completing my course?

By answering these questions, you will have a better idea of what to include in your course statement. Do not stress yourself out by trying to summarize everything about your course in a few sentences. Just cover a few of the key points. The same logic applies to what you will cover in your course. You have to separate the important from the unimportant because there is no way you will be able to teach every facet of your topic.

Logical Learning Sequences

Before designing your syllabus, consider how students learn in addition to what they will learn. Teachers no longer force-feed information to students. Rather, learning is a shared responsibility between students and teachers. A one-size-fits-all approach no longer functions. Demographics have changed and so have the job skills that are in demand.

Keep in mind that it is easier to learn when simple concepts are introduced first. Then you can build upon this basic information and expand into topics that are more complex. After you have established a logical presentation of your course information, you can begin thinking about how students will apply the information they learn. Again, remember that students can only apply higher-level thinking skills once they have mastered the basics.

Benjamin Bloom's Taxonomy, a chart for categorizing cognitive skills, is a good way to illustrate this point.

Bloom's Taxonomy

Knowledge

Recalling information, observation
Understanding key concepts
Skills: Listing, defining, describing, collecting, quoting

Comprehension

Understanding information and meaning
Interpreting, comparing, and contrasting facts
Skills: Summarizing, describing, prediction, associating, estimating

Application

Using information
Applying methods and concepts to new situations
Using skills and knowledge to solve problems
Skills: Calculating, applying, illustrating, modifying, experimenting

Analysis

Recognizing patterns and hidden meanings
Identifying key components
Skills: Analyzing, explaining, classifying, arranging, comparing

Synthesis

Making generalizations from facts
Relating knowledge from several topics

Making predictions and drawing conclusions
Skills: Modifying, rearranging, creating, designing, and composing.

Evaluation

Comparing ideas
Assessing the value of the information
Using reasoning to make argument
Skills: Assessing, ranking, testing, recommending.

TEACHER'S TIP:

Remember that teaching is more than
giving information to your students. It is an
interactive experience.

Some theories say there are two different types of learners: intrinsic and extrinsic. Students who are intrinsic are motivated by their desire to succeed. Intrinsic learners might reach higher levels faster because of their self-motivation and craving for learning.

Extrinsic learners might need an intellectual push or two from someone else. They are relying on you to help them set their achievement. In other words, other people motivate extrinsic learners. In either case, students must understand why they need to learn the material you are teaching.

Course Objectives

The backbone of your course will rest on your course objectives. These are statements that define everything your course is about. It tells students what they will be expected to learn and what they will be able to perform. If an activity or assignment is not in your course objective, you should toss it out. Write the course objective carefully, as everything you put into the objectives reflects the desired student outcome.

Sometimes it helps to look at the objectives in your textbook and then modify them to suit your course. Do not be afraid to ask for help from professional associations or your colleagues. You can also use the Internet to research syllabi of similar courses. Some sample syllabi are provided in the appendix of this book.

Designing the Syllabus

The syllabus is the framework for your course. It contains all of the basic information regarding the goals of the course, the parameters for measuring student performance, and a breakdown of the course load. Sometimes the syllabus is considered a contract between the teacher and his or her students. Include your contact information and your office hours so students are able to reach you for additional help outside of class time. Like your course statement, your syllabus is always a work in progress and should include a "subject to change" note in case planning needs to be adjusted during the semester. An example of a full course syllabus can be found in Appendix A, as provided by Professor Chad Lassiter of West Chester University of Pennsylvania.

Here are some common sections included in most syllabi:

The course

Include the course number, title, credit hours, semester, location, time, and dates for the class, and any prerequisites. Include a week-by-week schedule of what material will be covered so students get a feel for the pace of the course. These can include assignments, guest speakers, quizzes, and exams. Many instructors also place this information on their course Web sites.

Course materials

List the textbooks students will need to purchase for the entire length of the class, along with any additional materials they will be assigned to read. Include the International Standard Book Number (ISBN) number and edition number so students know they are purchasing the correct book. Be sure to list any materials or supplies required for your course, such as art materials, medical equipment, lab supplies, or computer software. You might want to list the hours for the campus libraries and any applicable labs that will help students complete their work.

Course requirements

One of the first sections students look at is the course requirements section. Here, a student can see your grading breakdown and what categories influence the student's grade, such as class participation, quizzes, and homework assignments. You might also include a section on classroom etiquette that lists rules regarding the use of electronics and respecting others when they offer their opinions or questions. Some colleges require this section in every syllabus.

Tardiness and absences

Even college students need to be reminded of the importance of being on time. Constant intrusions throughout a lecture distract you and your students. You might want to deduct points or penalize students who are chronically late. Some professors choose to lock the door once class begins. State your policy on absences as well. How many times may students miss class before it affects their grade? Some universities require student presence for a certain number of class hours to pass the course, so be sure to inform your students if they will be removed from the course for not attending.

Calendar of assignments

Outline what the assignments will be so students can prepare ahead of time. This will help students pace themselves so your class can operate as a unit, as well as keep you on track with your lectures. Grant yourself flexibility to change assignment due dates to allow for unforeseen problems or if your class needs to spend more time on a certain topic. Sticking to the schedule is not as important as student comprehension.

Missed exams or assignments

Let students know if they will be able to make up missed assignments or exams. Outline the criteria under which you will allow them to make it up, such as a serious illnesses or family emergency. You may require a doctor's note or some other form of proof that their absence was unavoidable. You may also place a limit on the number of times a student can miss assignments or exams.

Grading

Your students will worry most about your grading procedures. Show the breakdown of their entire grade in percentages, for example:

25% — Tests

20% — Quizzes and homework

15% — Class participation

25% — Final paper

15% — Attendance

Grading too harshly or too easily can mar your reputation or put your career on the line. Unless students are being tested via multiple choice, grading can be tricky. Talk to fellow professors to get an idea of what they regard as an "A" paper. An experienced professor can help you understand the criteria for grading everything from A to F, and will help you create rubrics for your grading systems. You will also gain insight into the pre-ferred grading policies of your institution from other professors.

Flexibility is another art to master. High standards are wonderful, but you might encounter groups of students — remember they are all different — who cannot keep pace. In these cases, you might consider grading on a curve if a large percentage of your students is not performing well.

TEACHER'S
TIP:

In addition to evaluating your students, take time for self-assessment. It can help improve your teaching, and there is always room for improvement.

Be sure to evaluate yourself, as well. Are large numbers of your students lazy, or are you not adequately covering all of the tested materials? Setting up students for failure is never a good idea for you or them. The goal is to teach students how to take their knowledge and apply it in real world situations, or to their chosen careers. At some point, your students will be tested and graded on how well they know the material you have presented, so aid them as much as possible without literally handing them the test in advance. This is called "teaching to the test;" this method is highly frowned upon and does not motivate students to remember and apply concepts.

At some point a student might say a test was unfair. You can avoid this by stating your grading policies up front. Outline how you will determine grades in your syllabus. During your course, give students tips on what will be tested. Grading can be both technical and subjective. That is why it helps to keep your own objectivity in check when it comes to grading.

Some educators recommend grading student work anonymously. Your preexisting opinion of a student might influence the grade you give him or her. Without knowing the student whose work you are grading, you can eliminate possible bias on your part. Have your students type their assignments so you cannot recognize handwriting, and have them include a cover sheet with their name and other information that you can easily ignore until you have read and graded the assignment.

Traditionally, college grades are given in letters. Other methods of grading include pass or fail, where students will receive a grade of either "P" or "F," a "P" indicating performance at a "D" level or higher. Work below the "D" level will constitute an "F." Auditing is another option that is sometimes offered at community colleges and other institutions that allow senior citizens or others to take classes for enrichment purposes. No grade is given. In accordance, classes taken as audit cannot be used toward graduation requirements. The classes might be tuition-free or charged at the regular tuition rate.

Plagiarism and cheating

A syllabus needs a brief statement about policies on plagiarism and cheating. Look at plagiarism and cheating simply in terms of what you should include in your syllabus. Some teachers emphasize this area of the syllabus because of the severe consequences related to plagiarism and cheating. Make it clear to your students that dishonesty can damage or end their academic careers. At the very least, it becomes a part of their academic records, making it difficult to apply to other colleges.

Colleges often have a zero-tolerance stance
toward plagiarism. Make sure your syllabus
clearly states the policy.

Make it clear that mistakes are not tolerated in this area. Most institutions will not accept the excuse that a student "forgot" to attribute the information. Tell your students to make sure to double-check any information they have cut and pasted from the Internet. An honest mistake can happen this way, but it is lethal to their academic careers, nonetheless.

Because of the levity carried by offenses involving cheating or plagiarism, the written policy is proof that students have been placed "on notice" that certain behaviors will not be tolerated. It specifies that plagiarism or cheating will have major consequences, including permanent expulsion from the college. Always follow college procedures once you are aware one of your students has cheated or plagiarized.

Stress the serious consequences of cheating.
Students that cheat or plagiarize risk creating
a negative record that other colleges and
even employers can access.

For more information about plagiarism and cheating, and what to do if it occurs in your classroom, see Chapter 15.

Chapter 4

Choosing the Best Textbooks

Choose a textbook that will enhance your students' understanding of the course subject. The right textbook can make the class soar; the wrong one can muddle what you are teaching. Check out reviews of a textbook before you select it for your class. There are sites that specialize in text book review, such as **www.rateitall.com**, but keep in mind that all reviews are opinions. Just because a book did not work for one professor does not necessarily mean it cannot work for you; however, such reviews can be a good indication.

At some colleges and universities, bookstores and administrative staff offer textbook guidelines for faculty. The final decision, however, rests with the teacher. Once you have your textbook, how you use it is also up to you. Remember, it is only one resource for your students. Feel free to mix and match the information as you choose. You can skip over chapters or present them in an order that best suits the sequence of your course. Use outside research to supplement the textbook. Do not have students read a lot of material that you are not going to cover. Give them the opportunity to ask questions or discuss what they read in small groups, if appropriate.

TEACHER'S
TIP:

Your textbook is only one resource for your course.
There is no need to follow it word-for-word.

Textbook Prices

For some students, the biggest issue with textbooks is the price, even if they qualify for financial aid. Get ready for complaints if you require a costly book that is not an integral part of your course, or worse, is rarely used. They also might not appreciate being asked to buy a textbook that you wrote. While there is nothing wrong with using a book you wrote for your class, be aware of the first impression it might give your students. They might think you are simply trying to make money off them. Students will most likely be satisfied if your textbook is effective and not overpriced.

Publishers are required to let faculty know at what price they sell their books to the college bookstore. Additionally, publishers must provide copyright dates for all textbook editions, descriptions of "substantial content revisions," and whether the material is available in other formats. They also must list the price of the other formats. All of this information must be provided in writing. The ISBN must be disclosed, along with the retail price. Materials that are sold as bundled packages must also be available individually. Do your research and see if you really need the latest edition of a book, or if an older and cheaper edition is just as informative.

Effective Textbook Use

Now we will look at some ways to use the textbook so students get the best learning experience and best value for their money. Exercises done before, during, and after reading can really enhance learning. For example, discuss an upcoming chapter in your class and ask students questions about the topic. Based on the discussion, make a list of key vocabulary words that might stump your students. You might even offer a list of key concepts they should glean from their reading. Encourage students to get the most from what they are reading by writing down questions as they go. When students ask questions while reading, it can lead to deeper learning.

One way students can do this is by thinking of questions for classroom discussions. As they progress through the chapters, ask them to connect information from previous chapters. Ask them to continually assess what they are learning through the textbook and why it is important. Students having difficulties with the material can write down questions about why it is hard for them to learn.

In contrast to effective uses of a textbook are ineffective uses. If students are reading chapters that never come up in class, they might cut corners by skipping the reading entirely. In many ways, the least effective textbook is the one that is never read.

Electronic Books

Electronic books are a growing trend in recent years. **Amazon.com** offers the Kindle, a hand-held device that holds uploaded digital versions of books, allowing students an alternative to carrying traditional college textbooks. Kindle is not yet a threatening force against traditional textbooks due to issues like limited textbook availability, its inability to display color images, and high cost. But, it is certainly a force to consider. Such devices make textbooks easier to cart around. If these devices grow in popularity, the college where you teach could eventually require them for all classes.

The Princeton University Press is one of the first academic publishing companies to delve into the electronic book market. In a small fall debut, the Press offered *The Subprime Solution: How Today's Global Financial Crisis Happened, and What to Do about It*, an economics book by Robert Shiller. The Princeton University Press plans to publish hundreds more books on the device, and the University of California offers a few dozen, with plans to publish others.

Teaching Without a Textbook

Just as it is not wise to base an entire course on a textbook, you might want to gain some experience before deciding to forgo a textbook. Textbooks are beneficial for beginning teachers as they present a logical order of material and can give you ideas about what your students should be learning. Looking through textbooks can also give you ideas about what to teach.

Some studies indicate that textbooks do not fit well with how students learn. Students also tend to regard their textbooks as a form of encyclopedia, rather than a teaching tool. Earlier, we learned how devices such as the Kindle seek to replace standard textbooks. There is other technology that might not completely replace textbooks, but can be used as a supplement or alternative to presenting information. Unlike electronic books, using technology in teaching is a trend that has already taken a strong hold in college campuses. In the next chapter, we will cover some of the ways you can use technology to supplement your lectures.

Chapter 5

High-Tech Learning

While you are planning the design of your course, think about how to use technology in your teaching. For example, you could require students to use at least three types of technology when giving oral reports. Technology must be considered in college courses because it is how we get most of our information in everyday life. It defines the way we communicate. Students and others live their lives through their cell phones and laptops. They are almost unable to disconnect from text messaging and e-mail. It seems technology is fast becoming a substitute for phone calls or face-to-face conversations. Whether you believe it is good or bad, it looks like technology is here to stay.

Technology has become firmly rooted in the classroom, as well. In K-12 education, technology in the classroom is not only an expectation, it is a federal requirement under the No Child Left Behind Act. Technology is no less important in postsecondary education. In recent years, institutions have created technology administrative positions to ensure technology is a key part of the programs. Older colleges have sometimes struggled with implementing technology, as their buildings were not built to support it. That is not the only challenge colleges have faced. Others include a lack of support from administrators, teachers who are not adept at technology, questions about how to assess if technology helps learning, and lack of technical support for using and maintaining technology in the classroom. Funding is another issue. Your college might not have the money to bring its classroom technology up-to-date. If that is the case, you might be able to apply for grants for learning and using new technology.

Another way colleges can raise money is through bond referendums, meaning that the college receives money from the public. These are not popular, especially during a down economy. But, asking taxpayers to fund projects might be the only way to make wholesale improvements on campus.

TEACHER'S TIP:

Technology is not only important in the classroom, its use is a skill sought after by your students' future employers.

Technology is as important to students as to the employers they will seek jobs from after they graduate. Even if someone works outside the realm of computer technology, they might still be expected to write blogs, search social networking sites, and conduct online marketing by using "keywords" in the copy they write. For example, a company might want someone to write a blog to help establish that person as an expert in a certain field. Being able to operate word processing programs, search the Internet, and e-mail are no longer considered coveted skills. They are expected.

Students cited campus technology as a high priority in their school selection, according to a 2008 study conducted by CDW Government Inc., an Illinois-based company that sells technology equipment to schools and government agencies. CDW surveyed more than 1,000 college students, technology staffers, and faculty for the study. The study found only 33 percent of faculty said technology is fully implemented on their campuses.

That included student access to technologies such as podcasts, video conferencing, and Web conferences.

The study also found approximately 42 percent of faculty use technology in every class. Another finding noted college students want chat sessions with their teachers, but only about 23 percent of institutions offered this.

Not surprisingly, one of the biggest barriers was a lack of knowledge about how to use technology. Using equipment you are not familiar with can lead to frustration for you and your students. Today's students grew up surfing the Internet and texting their friends. These students are going to be in your classroom, possibly coupled with some older students who are returning to college to finish or further their education. Students' varying skill levels can make it tricky for new college teachers to design lessons. You must have lessons that appeal to students who are both experts and novices at using technology.

CASE STUDY: USING TECHNOLOGY IN THE CLASSROOM

Steve Cunningham
Lecturer of music industry instruments/expertise
University of Southern California

Using technology in the classroom seemed natural for Steve Cunningham, a lecturer of music industry instruments and expertise at the University of Southern California. Cunningham got his first computer in 1978 and worked as a professional musician from the early to mid-1980s. A keyboard player by trade, Cunningham learned how to use synthesizers and then went on to build audio digital workstations.

He started teaching part-time at USC in 1998. "It started with one class, and I kind of liked it," Cunningham said. "Then I got up to about three classes as a part-timer, when I suddenly discovered — to be perfectly blunt — that one of the benefits of being a full-time faculty was that you could send one of your offspring to school for free. It was the deal of a lifetime. So, I began teaching full-time."

Perhaps because of his background with technology, Cunningham has made efforts to include new media in his courses. He has his students make a Facebook page, citing a study at Ohio State, where preliminary research showed students who have a Facebook page have higher grades. He also uses Twitter to illustrate the importance of communicating quickly through social networking.

"It is one of the first examples I give them if they have a show to promote. If someone is promoting a music show and they want to set aside a block of 20 tickets for VIPs, what happens is some of them might cancel at the last minute. Suddenly, four hours before the show, they would have several seats that need to be sold very quickly. The promoter then gets on Twitter and says, 'I've got 12 seats tonight for the Flaming Fenders, call me here, or follow this link to buy the tickets.' The tickets can be sold very quickly," Cunningham said.

Cunningham utilizes slideshows and online Web chats in his courses. The Web chat helps him include guest lecturers, who might be located too far from the classroom, in his course. With a computer set up at the guest lecturer's studio, students are able to ask him or her questions through Web cam software.

Cunningham said that when using slideshows in the classroom, however, instructors must remember not to over-pack their presentations. "I have read and taken to heart the book Death By PowerPoint. It lays out some guidelines for how to prevent boring your audience. For example, if you are going to do a PowerPoint, keep it to one idea per slide and preferably make it just a gem of the idea," Cunningham said. "Everyone can read on a projector and it is not necessary for you to read for them. Graphics are far more useful. You can also use embedded movie files and a lot of other stuff."

Building Teamwork With Technology

A recurring theme in the advantages of technology-based lessons is their ability to build teamwork or a sense of community among students. Courses are essentially learning communities. One portion is the instructor helping students; the other is students helping each other. It is difficult for students to work together and get to know each other in a traditional lecture setting. The opposite is true of online learning environments. The teacher and students can discuss things when they have an opportunity.

Contact is usually made on Weblogs, where students can post questions for the teacher and each other. For this format to be successful, however, students will probably have to be required to make posts on the site. In other words, they will need to do it for course credit.

Assessing Student Technology Skills

More than likely, your students will be savvy when it comes to technology. It is important to get a feel for how skilled your students are in technology before setting them loose on a major project, however. Do not expect them to succeed at setting up a Wiki page or Web site if they do not have these basic skills. For group projects, it is not always necessary that every student have every skill. By scouting out who can do what, it will make it easier to assign student leaders for technology projects.

Your role as a teacher is to create a balance between learning and technology. In other words, the use of technology must be meaningful. As you develop your skill in using technology in the classroom, you will be able to use more of it throughout the length of your course.

As a first-year teacher, you might need some training on using technology in the classroom. Be sure to take advantage of any training or guidance that your institution offers. You will likely find a wide range in your colleagues' technology skills. If you can find a fellow teacher who is good at using technology in the classroom, enlist that person as a mentor. Similar to your colleagues, you will find that your students will have varying levels of technology skills.

Many students use their computer for communicating with friends, checking e-mail, or doing research on the Internet. Others can build a Web page, post their own blogs, and download and upload photos, music, or movies. Fewer students understand computer networking or correcting problems on their own computers.

Even if your class is not technology-based, there are basic functions every student should be able to do. Students should be able to use today's computer programs, as well as understand and explain how technology works, along with its applications and limitations. Anything you can do to boost your students' skills in these areas will increase their marketability to future employers. These basic skills help with job readiness. They are also a foundation for building new skills.

As you are about to see, abstract thinking and technology were made for each other. If you are creatively inclined, you might find working with technology a lot of fun. Before choosing which media to use, answer the following questions based on what you want your students to learn:

- What are the learning objectives and teaching strategies for this lesson?

- How will the sequence of the activities your students will perform be set up, or what materials do you have that allow students to establish their own sequences?

- What types of media are needed for your learning objectives?

- Do you know how to use the media? Do the media match your teaching strategy?

- Do the media match student characteristics?

- Do the media match the learning environment?

- Did you select media that allow students to participate in learning activities?

- Does this type of technology work for your class overall, and what kinds of activities do you have in mind?

Here are some additional questions to consider:

- Is instructor and student interaction required through use of this technology?

- Will students have to be observed by the instructor as they perform a task?

- Is special equipment needed?

- Do students need to interact or collaborate with each other?

Easy Technology Projects

When using technology, creativity counts. But, how you use it does not have to be elaborate or cumbersome. Some teachers have virtual office hours so they can talk with students. They set up Wiki pages for student work online. They design Web sites that highlight student writing or art. Here are some creative ways other teachers have used technology:

- Holding online chat sessions. Do this the night before exams so students can get answers to last-minute questions.

Setting up a Web site to display student work. This works particularly well with English classes.

Using Wikis, a software program that allows the creation of a Web site where people can go to make contributions to or edit content. Wikis can be used in college classes quite easily, whether for assignments or for creating a community where students can communicate. More information is available at **http://wiki.org/wiki.cgi**. In addition to collaborating, Wikis are good tools for note taking and creating online communities.

- Blogging. Create a topic and allow students to discuss it online. It helps increase communication between students.

- Podcasting. Make an assignment that requires students to make a podcast (an audio report) instead of writing a paper. Have the students upload their podcasts to a Web site. Make sure your students have a computer with a microphone and audio software, or access to this equipment.

- Video conferencing. Use it to connect students to experts or guest speakers around the globe.

Do Not Fear the MP3 Player

Technology has the potential to change the way students learn and how they are taught. There is no reason to fear MP3 players such as the Zune, iPhone®, or iPod® because, in some cases, they can help learning. At Houston Community College, teachers found that students with iPhones spent more time studying when compared to those who used desktop computers. The experiment took place in an Anatomy and Physiology II class that combined a traditional classroom with distance learning, according to the Chronicle of Higher Education.

Under the experiment, students met once every week in person. The rest of their time was spent watching lecture videos and completing online assignments. Students were split into two groups of 20 each. Half the students had iPhones on loan from the college and the rest of the students did not. Using journals, students recorded the time they spent on the course, where they logged in, and when they logged in. The students with iPhones used small breaks in their day to spend time studying. The iPhone students also formed study groups more quickly. It was not clear whether a fascination with a new technology is what led the students with iPhones to study more. One thing did appear certain: it helped students connect with each other.

Houston Community College is not the only institution to use this technology. Several other colleges — Oklahoma Christian University, the University of Maryland, Abilene Christian University in Texas and Freed-Harmon — are planning to use iPhones and iPods for incoming students, according to the International Herald Tribune, the international version of the New York Times. Part of the reason the devices are popular is how light and less bulky they are to carry around than a laptop computer. Some of the colleges are approaching the usage of the devices in class like an experiment. They are giving out iPhones and iPods to small groups of students to see how they use the technology. It is not free for students, either. Those who use the iPhones must purchase their own telephone service for the devices if they wish to use them as cell phones.

There are several things to consider before suggesting that students should purchase their own devices. If you have a high number of low-income students, they might not be able to afford it. You can always require the purchase as part of your course. Check with your department first, especially if no instructor has ever asked students to purchase iPhones and iPods.

As faddish and fun as it seems, not everyone is jumping on the technology bandwagon. Some teachers are refusing to jump on at all. For example,

Cornell Law School teacher Robert Summers banned laptop computers from his classroom, according to the New York Times.

Summers, a 40-year teaching veteran, was annoyed by the constant tip-tapping of students typing on their laptop keyboards. He did not think they were focusing enough on what was going on in the classroom. In his opinion, students must learn to think with their own brains, and not use a computer as a supplement. Whether you agree with this position or not, it offers the ultimate lesson in using new or existing technology. It must benefit learning.

Online Learning

There is a good chance you will be asked to teach an online class at some point. It could even be a large portion of the classes you teach. Entire degree programs ranging from associate's degrees to master's degrees might be completed online. All other aspects of the class, from office hours to lectures and tests, are also being done online. The biggest difference for an online teacher is deciding how best to get students the information they need without the use of a lecture hall. This can be done by posting text, assignments, videos, and other materials on the Internet. Even if you are not teaching entirely online, you can use these same techniques in a regular classroom.

CASE STUDY: A NEW WAY OF TEACHING

Tim Serey
Adjunct professor, organizational behavior, adult development & life planning, and organizational leadership
Ashford University and
The University of the Rockies

Tim Serey retired from teaching college in the late 1990s, but his work was far from over.

As a 20-year veteran of traditional professoring on campus, Serey immediately missed teaching after his retirement. He ended up teaching at three online schools, and in 2006, he discovered the high standards of integrity and professionalism at the University of the Rockies and Ashford University. The values of these universities were in line with his own, which immediately allowed Serey to connect to the online schools on a personal level.

Since then, Serey has continued to play a role in the continued growth of online universities, a demand that is growing worldwide. In fact, many prestigious universities — both private and public — are offering a range of programs online, and the quality of these programs continues to improve. Ashford University, for example, has met the same standards from the Council on Higher Education as the nation's leading universities, Serey said.

Online universities are also becoming more prominent because of the convenience they offer. Students can log onto classes when their schedules permit them to, rather than being constrained by a course schedule, Serey pointed out. Others see the convenience as a benefit because they are able to register for classes at a particular university even if they do not live in that region. "This is a particular advantage for military personnel abroad, and even those aboard ships at sea," Serey said.

But while online universities make the lives of students easier, that is not always the case for those who teach the classes. Often, teaching remotely involves more work for the professors in comparison to the amount of work that is put into campus lectures and courses. Part of the effort, Serey said, comes from having to maintain contact with students. Because there is no chance for face-to-face contact online, professors have to work harder to communicate with students, as they often take extra steps to touch base with them. It gets harder — online professors, like Serey, have to use that communication to convey their expertise in a subject, while being careful not to come across with a "know-it-all" attitude.

Connecting with students on an emotional level is a whole other ball game. Because this type of connection is essential for creating an atmosphere that facilitates online, higher-level learning, instructors have to present themselves as they really are, writing to convey emotion and intensity through their remote contact with students. "Online instructors who convey this breathe life into the adage that people soon forget what we tell them, but long remember how we make them feel," Serey said.

The main difference in this, Serey said, comes in the fact that many online professors see themselves as a coach instead of as a traditional teacher who stands in front of a group and lectures. By using e-mail, online instructors can act as individualized coaches for their students, providing feedback to the students in a constructive, coach-like manner. For those who do not want to correspond via e-mail, or who want a more personal touch, home or cell phone numbers are provided, Serey said.

While some professors may see this type of individualized contact as a hassle, or even a problem, Serey said he can easily point out the benefit: being able to help students who are shy. In traditional classrooms, shy students often do not ask for help even though they need it, and their questions go unanswered and unnoticed by professors lecturing to hundreds at a time. But, with remote classes, Serey said that it is easier for teachers to pick up on those students who seem to be having a hard time understanding the material. So, instead of waiting for the shy student to seek the professor's help, the professor can take notice of a low grade and contact the student, asking if he or she needs help.

The shyness factor works both ways, however. Serey said that since he has been teaching online, he feels more free to be himself, showing his sense of humor from time to time. Now, when things go awry or he makes a mistake, Serey is able to laugh at himself and move forward, something that was not easily done in a traditional setting.

For Serey, teaching online has affected nearly every level of how he teaches. "There is no question that I am a better teacher, and more empathetic toward my students," he said. "As a result of teaching online, I work much harder at teaching than ever before, spending much more time on helping students."

Tim Serey has been a college professor for 33 years. He has published more than 15 articles and has received numerous awards, including the Professor-in-Residence award for The Kroger Company and Ashford University's Provost's Circle Award for teaching excellence. He currently teaches undergraduate and doctoral-level courses about Organizational Behavior and Leadership at Ashford University and the University of the Rockies.

Even though online courses are in demand, they might not be popular with all faculty members because of the additional work they require. Alternatively, you might also be asked to convert an existing class into an online version. This can be a time-consuming task, depending on the subject matter.

The absence of formal lectures presents yet another challenge. There are several ways to make up through lost lecture time by using a Web site, including:

Text

All of your lecture notes can be placed online. It might not be as flashy, but students can read much faster than they can listen to an hour-long presentation. You can also include links to articles that are available online. If you use a textbook for your traditional classroom, make sure to use it for the online class, too. You can also add documents to enhance lessons, such as lists of key topics for study, examples of "A" work, and supplemental reading material.

Slideshows

This is a relatively easy way to present information online. There are many software programs that make it easy for you to record your voice while clicking through the slides. These programs then generate the slideshow into a format that can be posted on the Internet. There is much opportunity in adding graphics to these slideshows. Visual representations of data can help students who struggle to understand a topic in writing.

Podcasts

Podcasts are digital audio or video files — typically audio files — available for download. These podcasts can be downloaded for free, and your students can even upload and save them using iTunes®. For more information about podcasts, visit **www.apple.com/itunes/podcasts.** You can create a podcast series based on important sections of your lectures or your lectures in their entirety. A recording of your voice is easy to create with a few pieces of equipment, and can emphasize key points that you want to make. You can also direct students to download podcasts from other sources to supplement their learning. News and research organizations often provide podcasts of stories or issues, and Web sites such as **www.LearnOutLoud. com** offer lists of podcasts, both free and paid. Because students are able to download a podcast, they can listen to it as many times as they need. They are also able to rewind sections they might struggle to understand or review before tests or large projects.

Videos

High-quality Web cams (a computer device that captures images and can send live video to and from connected computers), digital cameras, and video recorders are relatively inexpensive and easy to use. You can use them to make recordings or live videos. One way to use videos is to introduce students to your class before the semester starts. It gives them a chance to see your face, even if it is not in person. You can also record your lectures or experiments to visually illustrate topics to your students. Also, videos can be used in the same way as podcasts to supplement learning. You can provide links to videos you want your students to watch, or require them to make video presentations. This can also be done for free through You-Tube™, **www.youtube.com**, by creating an account and uploading your video. YouTube also allows you to type in a description of your video, along with a list of key terms to help your video show up in the searches conducted by other YouTube users.

Group projects

When assigning group projects online, make sure the task is clearly defined before implementing such a project as a teaching strategy. These projects can include writing group papers, creating Wikis (a Web site that allows users to edit or create Web pages) or Web sites related to a specific topic, or any project that fits with the course. Students can meet either in person or use text or video chat to discuss and plan the project. This can help students develop precise communication skills and learn from each other. The projects can then be uploaded to the class Web site so students can view and learn from each other's work.

Quizzes

"Open book" or self-correcting quizzes online can help students learn. These are quizzes that either allow students to research the answers as they take the quiz, or that will automatically mark the answer wrong when the student answers incorrectly. They work best if you include background information that explains the correct answers on the Web site being used to take the quiz. These quizzes are intended to get students thinking about the material — they are not used to evaluate their performance. Sample quizzes can also be used to assist students in reviewing before tests. Quiz- and test-making software can be purchased, but can also be found for free online. Regardless of what program you use to make an online quiz, you may want to explore your options with a free program like the one at **www. proprofs.com/quiz-school**.

Posting comments

Design a question or mini writing assignment and allow students to answer it online. Then, instruct students to read postings made by several other students and comment on each one. This helps to direct discussions so the comments are not random. Consider giving students credit for posting comments and commenting on topics that other students have written about. If you do not make it count, your students will be less likely to devote quality time to posting comments.

Online meetings

If your schedule allows, consider holding office hours online. You could hold chat room sessions in which students can pose questions and receive answers in real time. These sessions can also be used to help with review before major tests. You could also set up video or audio sessions with students. You can post the date and times of these sessions on the course Web site, or send out e-mail reminders so interested students can choose whether they wish to "attend" via cyberspace. You can also record these online sessions if you need to refer back to them at a later date.

Problems with Online Learning

Every teaching method has its drawbacks, and the same is true of online courses. Web sites can crash, leaving students unable to access the materials they need. Ask if your college has a help desk or other resources to assist students having minor problems with their courses. If this service is not available, provide students with alternative ways to get answers to questions, such as researching the Internet or looking through their textbooks.

One of the biggest drawbacks a first-year teacher can face with online courses is time. Developing a traditional course is hardly a fast and easy project. Designing and developing an online course can take even more time.

Yet another time-related constraint is change. Technology is constantly changing, and the course you develop this year will no doubt face modifications. Changes in curriculum or college policies can influence the content of your course. This is really no different from traditional classrooms. Teachers are constantly assigning new reading materials based on recent articles or textbooks. Similarly, online teachers must continually update the multimedia they are using.

Do not expect to be offered any additional pay for putting extra effort into an online course. In a survey of faculty at colleges and universities, the National Education Association found faculty teaching online or distance learning classes often have more students and work longer hours.

Without the restrictions of the four walls of the classroom, it can be tempting for administrators to pack students into Web-based courses. Yet class sizes need to be limited to allow proper communication between teachers and students. Obviously, larger classes require more time for coordinating message boards, chat rooms, and other online functions that are done as a group. Large classes can also fill your e-mail inbox with student questions. It takes time to read and respond to each message. Just like a traditional classroom, online teachers need time to give feedback to students on their assignments. In fact, one of the criticisms of online learning is a lack of personal contact and guidance.

Instruction seems almost absent because students are much more self-directed. Teachers also lack the face-to-face interaction with students that allows them a greater understanding of whether or not their students are grasping the material. The key to getting around these problems is more communication online through e-mail and chat sessions. For this reason, it is more difficult to develop a relationship with individual students when you have a large class.

TEACHER'S TIP:

Online learning offers students the convenience of a flexible schedule that allows them to work whenever they want. Be aware that this can be a challenge for those who are not self-motivated.

Advantages and Disadvantages to Online Learning

From the flexibility of your schedule to the minimal traveling you will have to do, teaching your class, or classes, online can easily seem like the way to go. But, sprinkled within the many perks of remote classes are some disadvantages. Use the following list to help you weight the advantages and disadvantages of teaching online classes:

Advantages

Flexibility: There are no set times, so both you and your students can work whenever you want — for the most part.

Commute: The furthest you will have to travel is to your own computer, or maybe your home office.

Organization: You can store your lecture notes online so that students can access them any time.

Comfort: Unless you are doing video conferencing, no one else is going to see you, so your days of dressing professionally to establish your authority are over — you can even teach in your pajamas.

No wallflowers: Communication is open to all students, even those who are shy or who do not like to talk during class. This can result in increased learning and a higher success rate of your students.

Disadvantages

Discipline: Students who lack time management skills and self-discipline may find it difficult to actually do the work required by an online class.

Isolation: If you or your class thrives on interaction, online classes may present a challenge. Sometimes it is hard to strike up the same discussions that you can in a traditional classroom setting.

Access: If your students do not have access to a high-speed Internet connection, they are going to have problems accessing your course and the materials they need. Also, if students do not have a lot of experience with computers, they will have a harder time with the course than those who spend most of their time communicating online. This is because they will have to take more time to figure out how to work things like videos, how to participate in chat rooms or discussions, or how to download attachments.

What Works and What Does Not Work

As more and more teachers at all levels put their course materials online, other teachers are learning what works and what does not.

1. **Keep unit sizes small.** Do not be tempted to put too much information on your Web site. Several assignments are enough. Also, keep the unit sizes roughly the same for all your courses. This way, students get an idea of what your assignments are like.

2. **Provide adequate instructions.** Tell students what to do and why they are doing it. This can help prepare them for future assignments, quizzes, and tests that build on the material.

3. **Have a mix of self-study and teacher-corrected assignments.** It provides a variety of challenges and helps keep students interested.

4. **Post questions and quizzes on the course Web site.** This way, students do not have to go to another site to write their answer. They are more likely to finish the work if you keep them on the site. It is also easier for you to find the assignments and grade them.

5. **Pose questions and provide reading assignments.** It helps students focus on key points in the reading.

6. **Include due dates.** Have a listing right on your site that lists due dates for assignments.

7. **Be creative.** Some examples include assigning students to draw diagrams; write screenplays; and post short videos, slide shows, and photo essays. It helps break up writing assignments and quizzes. But do not go crazy with it. One creative assignment per unit is a reasonable goal.

Interaction, Not Isolation

Teaching a distance learning class offers many challenges to the teacher. You will have a large number of students with different learning styles. Distance learning will not offer the opportunity to get to know your students well, unlike classroom learning. With effective use of many forms of technology, however, you can still be successful. There are chat rooms, e-mail access, group discussion forums, videos, document submission software, and other ways for the teacher to reach out to online students.

Taking courses on the Internet or through videos allow adult students to work full-time and study at their own convenience. They might do better with online courses when compared to younger students, as older students might be more disciplined to deal with this level of freedom.

Laptops are great because all of your programs can go with you wherever you go. As for student assignments, you can only bank on the programs and equipment your college has to offer. Keep in mind that some of your students might not have access to a laptop or desktop computer. Their only access will be through the library or computer labs. Make sure all students are aware of hours and availability of campus computer labs. Unless you are teaching a design class that requires students to buy expensive software, it is best to keep your assignments fairly basic and hassle-free.

TEACHER'S TIP:

Not all of your students in traditional classes might have a computer. Make sure everyone is aware of computer lab hours and availability.

On the other hand, technology keeps advancing at a rapid pace. Skills that were considered to be cutting-edge a few years ago are now about as impressive as sending an e-mail. Skills like building basic Web pages and using computer graphic design programs, such as Photoshop or Flash, are not as unusual now as they were ten years ago. In the past, it was also acceptable to work with either a Macintosh or a Windows-based computer. Now, students must be able to move smoothly between both operating systems to be competitive in the workforce.

Whatever technology is used must complement the course and get students to interact. For example, using a PowerPoint presentation is not interactive. Message boards are interactive.

Finally, technology skills can be built upon during a semester, culminating in a final, creative project.

Chapter 6

First-Day Success

Preparation is the key for success on your first day of class. Set two alarm clocks and do not leave any detail unattended from the night before, such as packing your lecture notes or picking out your clothes.

As a student, you have already seen your share of the good, the bad, and the ugly teachers. It is normal to be a little apprehensive. You might start to question whether you can create the magic that some professors seem to make so effortlessly. You might wonder if your first class will fall flat.

TEACHER'S TIP:

Project a comfortable, yet professional image with your clothing choices.

Appearances are also important in first impressions. Someone's choice of clothing, hairstyle, and overall grooming greatly influence our opinion of them. Strike a balance between looking professional and being hip and comfortable. Cargo pants and flip-flops make you appear more like a surfer than a college teacher. A professional, yet casual image is best. It is better to err on the side of being frumpy rather than fashionable, according to *The*

Chronicle of Higher Education. A good rule of thumb is to observe what your colleagues are wearing. A graphic arts teacher, for example, has more flexibility than does someone teaching business classes.

Our clothing does send a message about who we are, and we want to make sure we are sending the right message.

Easing Anxiety

There is no reason to panic on your first day. After all, you arrived early to set up your classroom. You have spent a lot of time preparing your course by designing an effective syllabus. You are well-versed in college policies, and you are about to learn some easy, yet important ways to connect with your students.

TEACHER'S **TIP:**

Being well-prepared and organized will really reduce stress on your first day.

When the first day arrives, it is normal to be a little nervous. If you suspect your case of butterflies will be significant, practice some stress-reducing techniques well before the first day. The following are some helpful ways to reduce your anxiety:

1. **Focus on what you can do.** Do not let yourself get so caught up in worrying about what could go wrong that you forget your game plan. Focusing on what you plan to do is more productive and directs your thoughts to a positive place.

2. **Keep emotions in check.** What is really the worst thing that can happen? What are the chances of it happening? Applying logic to the situation can make it much less stressful.

3. **Create distractions.** Having a hobby can keep your mind off of needless worrying. After you thoroughly prepare for your class, allow your mind to relax by exercising, reading, or listening to music.

4. **Laugh it off.** If you stumble over your words or trip in front of the class, do not take it too seriously. Try to see the humor in situations. If something goes wrong, do not beat yourself up. The things that go wrong are often the things we do not anticipate. Get through it with humor and grace, and then move on.

5. **Set goals.** By setting small goals for preparing for class, you build your confidence along the way by accomplishing each one. Again, you are focusing your attention on something positive.

6. **Find a balance.** Being blindly optimistic can be as unhealthy as being totally cynical. How can excessive optimism cause stress? If you believe things will work out perfectly and they do not, it can create a lot of anxiety. The best approach is to be realistic.

7. **Seek out supportive people.** If possible, talk with other teachers to get some reassurance that the first day will not be as bad as your imagination is trying to make you believe. They lived through it and so will you.

8. **Arrive early.** This gives you time to organize your notes and set up any media equipment. It is also a good way to greet students as they begin arriving, and demonstrates that you are in control. You do not want to walk in at the last minute and be greeted by rows and rows of waiting and watching eyes. As

the semester progresses, continue arriving five minutes early. Students will use that time to ask you questions.

Introductions 10

From the first minute of class, begin working to establish a rapport with your students. Building rapport can be boiled down to one concept: Treating students with respect. If you are distant, arrogant, or play favorites, you will alienate some of your students and possibly hinder their learning.

Students are not impressed by your degrees or publications. They want a teacher who is down-to-earth, concerned with their success, reasonable, evenhanded, and respectful of their opinions.

TEACHER'S TIP:

Allowing students to introduce themselves can help them get to know each other and make you seem more approachable as a teacher. Even in an auditorium filled with students, encourage your students to take a few minutes at the beginning of class and introduce themselves to the people they are sitting next to.

Tell the students something about your life so they can relate to you as a person. You might tell them about a professor who inspired you to become a teacher. Mention your family members, your hobbies, and anything else that gives them a glimpse into your life. To give an impression of how you think, display a favorite quote on the whiteboard or chalkboard. Tell the students why the quote is important to you and how it relates to teaching or your views on life.

Here are some ideas that are not quite as time-consuming:

- Pass out a letter to each student that offers your biography, background, and your interests outside of the classroom.

- Ask every student to fill out an index card that lists his or her name, phone numbers, e-mail address, major, whether they work a full- or part-time job, and how they like to learn.

- An ongoing activity you can try is seeking out one student each day and attempting to learn something about him or her.

You might feel you are wasting time on the first day, but you are actually taking some key steps to build rapport and set your students (and yourself) on a course for success.

Mention that you are pleased to see everyone, and welcome the students to the class one more time. It is best for you to figure out exactly how you will introduce yourself. Think about this well in advance.

After the introductions, review the syllabus briefly. There is probably no need to spend an entire hour on this. However, you do want to give students a feel for what is expected. Five term papers, weekly quizzes, and a final exam that counts for half of the grade may not make students feel like celebrating, but they need to know what the expectations are going to be.

Breaking the ice

Cover the basics, then try an icebreaker activity. Icebreakers are a fun and interesting way for everyone to get to know each other. By allowing the class to interact with each other and see each other as individuals with valuable experiences, you have taken the first step toward building a sense of community. When students learn each other's names, it gives them a sense that there are others in their class with whom they can interact. This leads to more interactions and learning in and out of the classroom.

An icebreaker is simply a brief, fun activity that provides an opportunity for people to introduce themselves to each other. It is important because you want your class to function as a learning community. To do that, you cannot have a bunch of strangers in your classroom that never talk to each other. The following activities are only suggestions. Feel free to modify them as you see fit. Keep in mind that in a large, lecture hall-sized class, you will want to be sure you can maintain authority before starting an icebreaker with your students. Depending on the age of the students you have, you also may have to make an extra effort to keep icebreakers at a college-age level, although sometimes college students will enjoy the chance to joke around.

Activity No. 1

Ask students to introduce themselves to five other students. During the interview, they can ask questions about where the other people are from, why they chose to go to that college, and why they chose to take your course. If your class is small, you can even take a few minutes to go around the whole class and have each student share what they learned about another student.

Activity No. 2

If you are pressed for time, you might go around the room and ask each student what he or she hopes to learn in your class. Write down the most common categories and briefly discuss them with the class.

Activity No. 3

Ask students to move their chairs into a circle and run down a list of pre-determined categories. Some ideas for categories include living in another state, speaking more than one language, having brothers or sisters, being born outside the United States, playing a sport, experience traveling abroad, undecided major, knowing or being related to someone famous, having naturally blonde hair, and enjoying reality television. As you can see, the categories are limitless. If that category applies to a student they can raise their hand or stand up.

If you have a large class, you do not have to have the students move their chairs into a circle — they can stay in their seats. Also, with a large class, it will be easier and faster to have a predetermined list of characteristics that your students may have in common. You may also wish to choose some characteristics that you know will illicit laughter to ease the mood.

The Classroom is Your Stage

The concept of "acting" while doing something in everyday life can have a negative connotation. Acting as it refers to teaching is about entertaining. Did you ever have a teacher who stood in one place and droned on and on in a monotone voice? Assuming you stayed awake, you might recall that it was not too entertaining.

Students are more attentive in classrooms with teachers who are good entertainers. These teachers use dramatic gestures, exciting speech, and elements of surprise when they present information. These elements are more important than ever as we live in a world driven by exciting multimedia presentations.

The goal of both teachers and actors is to capture their audience's attention. As a teacher, you must first capture your students' attention so they can learn. Effective actors and teachers also use nonverbal communication to get their points across.

Not surprisingly, actors and teachers also have some of the same fears. They worry about blanking out and forgetting what they were supposed to say. They worry whether their audiences will accept them. And both groups are faced with the challenge of overcoming their fears and putting on their best performance. Two of the most important techniques teachers can use to prepare their best "act" are planning and enthusiasm. Actors study their lines. Teachers plan their course content and how they are going to present it.

Enthusiasm comes from a love of teaching and one's subject matter. But, there are also ways of conveying that enthusiasm in front of your class. Some of these include animated body movements, inflection in tone of voice, suspense, surprise, humor, role-playing, effective use of classroom space, and props. Making a grand entrance and exit are two more ways to convey enthusiasm. Additional factors to consider are nonverbal expressions and adapting to one's audience. Nonverbal expression includes physical movement, vocal variation, and facial expressions. Having a range of these skills allows teachers to emphasize certain points. Think of how boring it would be to watch a performance with actors who never move or change their facial expressions.

The whole world might be our stage, but for teachers, their stage mainly consists of the four walls that is their classroom. Use your classroom space as if it were a stage. Arrange the desks so there is maximum student visibility. Having students sit in ways where you can easily see them can also make it easier to learn their names. Learning names is yet another important part of your "performance."

Learning Student Names

TEACHER'S
TIP:

Learning student names adds a personal touch to your class, but be realistic. This works best in small classes, not giant lecture halls.

If you are teaching an auditorium of 300 students, it is going to be next to impossible to remember all of their names. You simply will not have the time to do it. Learning names is a more realistic goal for smaller classes of 20 to 40 students. That is not to say you cannot learn names in classes that are larger than that. Unfortunately, the personal touch can get lost in giant lecture halls, and one thing that suffers is being able to learn everyone's names. Still, the importance of attempting to learn names should not be diminished.

Learning your students' names might be more important than you think. Some educators say it is one of the most important exercises in building rapport. It is hard to appear warm and accessible if Jennifer comes up to you after class with a question and you cannot remember her name.

Knowing just a portion of your students' names can help create a more inviting atmosphere. For some teachers, this will be easy. Others will struggle. If you struggle, keep a positive attitude and start with learning the names of small groups of students. You can speed this along by asking everyone to sit in the same seats, at least in the early stages of your class.

Why is it so difficult for some people to remember names? When we are introduced to others, we might not be focused on remembering their name. The very first thing someone tells you is his or her name. By the time you have exchanged a few moments of conversation, you have already forgotten the other person's name.

Here are some tips to help avoid ever having to say, "What was your name again?"

- Repeat the person's name back to them, without emphasis, so it is not obvious that you are trying to remember it. If appropriate, repeat the name a couple of times throughout the rest of your conversation.

- Make up rhymes or alliterations inside your head that help you remember their name: Tall Tom, Bill the Pill, Merry Sherri…

- Spell the name backwards. This will make you concentrate on the name.

Chapter 7

Inside the Daily Classroom

The best way to find out what students know is to ask them. This gives you a chance to assess students and set the tone for the class. It sends a message that learning is something that is actively pursued. Asking students about what they already know also provides them with a way to self-assess their knowledge level and evaluate whether their information is accurate.

One way to do this is to have your students write answers to writing prompts or a series of prompts. A good way to start is with the opening "What do you know about…" Then have your students fill in the rest of the question as it relates to your course. For example, say you are teaching an introductory course about Shakespeare. Have your students read a passage and ask them to write down one thing they liked about it. In a government class, you could draw on various historical events and ask students how they would have reacted in those circumstances. Tell students not to worry if they are correct or not.

When they are finished, write their answers on the chalkboard or whiteboard. If another student challenges an answer during a group discussion, place a question mark next to it on your board. It is perfectly fine to write down incorrect answers as long as you take the time to explain why their answers were incorrect. After the students finish writing, have them form small groups and discuss their answers. The idea is to get students thinking by using what they already know. This helps to establish a base where they can attach and connect the new knowledge they are going to learn in your class.

In short, it tells you what your students know and it tells them what they know, as well.

It can develop a hunger for knowledge that will carry through your entire course. It teaches students to be active learners, rather than to sit back and hope that if they take notes and memorize the material, they will do well in your class. It also builds a sense of community in your class, a recurring theme for success.

If the exercise goes well, you can follow up by asking students what they learned from each other. All of the previous answers will be up on the board so your students can refer back to them.

Assessing What Students Already Know

There are some problems with this approach, however, and it might not always work well.

One of the difficulties is arguments between students during discussions. Do not allow extended disputes about whether an answer is right or wrong, but keep the discussion moving. If there is a wide range of knowledge levels, the students who are more advanced might not be so forgiving of classmates who are not as knowledgeable. The most knowledgeable students can also dominate the discussion and leave others little time to contribute.

This can also be intimidating to students with a limited background in your topic.

As the teacher, you can walk around the room and listen in on some of the discussions. If one person is dominating the discussion, have every student in the group tell you what they think. It is also possible that your topic will not lend itself well to this kind of discussion. It might help to teach students something and then have them do the exercise.

This exercise will not give you an in-depth view of every student's knowledge level. Rather, it will allow you to see the overall level of your class. It is an approach that can also be used to assess students before and after testing.

Another way to use the information gleaned from the exercise is to mention it throughout the course. Students can also do a form of self-assessment by looking at their lists. They can do this by comparing what they knew at the start of the class to what they are learning as the class progresses.

Lesson Plans

At the most basic level, lessons are carefully planned classroom activities with a specific goal for what you want your students to learn. It is not something that must be followed like a script. Leave room for spontaneity, as well the opportunity to toss out what does not work.

As you gain experience as a teacher, you will improvise more and add creativity to your lessons while you are in front of your class.

A good lesson plan describes what the teacher will do and say, as well as how students might respond. Teachers also try to anticipate the difficulties students might have in learning the material. Sometimes, creating a lesson plan can be done with other teachers. This gives teachers a chance to work directly with their peers and learn how to design effective lessons.

Essentially, teachers strive to base their lessons on how students are learning. They observe what the students are learning from the lesson and use that information to revise their lessons, if necessary. These practices are common in K-12 education and can also be used in postsecondary settings. One word of caution, however, is that it can be time-consuming.

For obvious reasons, it can be beneficial for a new teacher to work with veteran teachers.

You will be learning from others who have more experience than you. You will learn ways to design effective classroom activities. You will also gain a greater understanding of how to assess your students' progress. Studying a single lesson allows teachers to make improvements in student learning without overhauling an entire course.

Whether you have the opportunity to work in a group or must go it alone, here are some key principles to keep in mind when designing a college curriculum:

- Your curriculum should be clearly linked to your institution's mission statement.

- Design your own mission statement and goals for your curriculum. List what you expect students to learn after completing your course. (This is also a part of your course syllabus).

- Design and choose student activities from researched-based methods.

- Use a logical sequence for presenting educational activities.

- Continually assess and strive to improve the curriculum.

Keep in mind there will be variations in your curriculum based on what courses students decide to take. The institution sets a sequence of courses that it wants students to take, but students might choose not to take all of the courses, or they might not take them in the proper order. It is helpful to monitor which courses your students are actually taking. This can influence whether students will achieve the expected outcome from your course. Advising students allows you to assess their goals. The best academic advising allows students to reach their goals within the confines of the institution's expectations for what they should learn.

SAMPLE LESSON PLAN AND WEEK OUTLINE

Courtesy of Professor Chad Lassiter, West Chester University
Race Relations, Course SWO 225
Undergraduate Department of Social Work

"Of all the civil rights for which the world has struggled and fought for five thousand years, the right to learn is undoubtedly the most fundamental"—W.E. B. Du Bois

Outline - Week 4

1. Listen to Nina Simone's song

2. Give explanation of Nina Simone's song

3. White Privilege discussion- Yellow Book

4. White Privilege defined- PowerPoint

5. Discovering My Whiteness- PowerPoint

6. Helms Identity Model- PowerPoint

7. Lecture on Healy- p. 1-138

8. Lecture on Tatum

9. Us and Them Lecture- "No Promise Land" p. 22-30-
    Reading Leaders

    Describe the mutual intolerance between Mormons and Missouri-
    ans. What stereotypes the two groups believe about one another?
    Group #1

    Was segregation effective in preserving the peace between Mor-
    mons and other Missourians? Explain. **Group #2**

    Why did Missourians try to deny Mormons the vote? **Group #3**

    In what ways were the Mormons' religious freedoms violated?
    Group #4

    There were many warning signs that the dispute between Mor-
    mons and Missourians was going to turn violent. What warn-
    ing signs might you look for in your school or neighborhood,
    and what strategies can be used to avert violence between the
    groups? **Group #5**

10. A Place at the Table Lecture- "This Land is Ours" p. 44, and "Against
    the Current" p. 98 - **Reading Leaders**

11. Us and Them Lecture- "Blankets for the Dead"- p.14

    In what ways did the Cherokees try to conform to European ideas
    of civilization? Why? **Group #5**

    How does the "roots/potatoes" incident highlight cultural bias?
    Group #2

    What is the tone of the letter from Choctaw Chief George Harkins?
    What is his attitude toward the government's policy of Indian
    removal? **Group #4**

    Why did the U.S. government continue to view Indians as a prob-
    lem, even after The Trail of Tears? What strategy would the govern-
    ment use next? **Group #1**

Describe the Indian removal from north Georgia. Was the evacuation carried out according to plan? Explain. What were the holding camps like? Why did many Indians choose to walk rather than ride the boats the government provided? **Group #3**

11. Collect Family of Origin Paper

12. Close out class and state what we will be going over next class

Class format

4:15-5:45	**1st part of class**
5:45-6:00	**Break**
6:00-7:00	**2nd part of class**
7:00	**Class over**

Professor Chad Lassiter is nationally recognized for his work with resilient and vulnerable families, youth, and communities. With a Masters degree from the University of Pennsylvania Graduate School of Social Work, Lassiter concentrates on the fields of American race relations and violence prevention among African American males, and has worked on two national research projects: P.L.A.A.Y. (Preventing Long-term Anger and Aggression in Youth) and H.I.P.P. (Health Information Providers and Promoters). Turn to Appendix A *to see Lassiter's sample syllabus.*

Lassiter has also worked on race, peace, and poverty-related issues in Africa and Israel. He has been named as one of Philadelphia's Most Influential African Americans, 10 People Under 40 to Watch in 2005, and has won various awards for his community service, including the Dr. Martin Luther King, Jr. Community Involvement Award in 2008. With lists of other awards and recognitions, Lassiter is able to use his experience and acknowledgements to bring real-life lessons to his students at West Chester University in a credible manner.

Defining Outcomes

Defining what students should learn from the curriculum can help set the course for how and what the faculty teaches. As already mentioned, setting curricular goals and objectives helps provide a foundation for what students should learn. It also offers direction for assessing whether or not students are learning. When the curriculum sets the goals and objectives, the temptation to teach to a test is diminished.

There are also areas to avoid when assessing if students are achieving their learning goals, including:

- Reducing expectations or "dumbing down" the material when the expected outcomes are not achieved.

- Grade inflation, the practice of giving students a higher grade than what is really deserved. Inflating grades can result in a lack of effort by faculty and students. It can potentially devalue the degrees that students earn, as well.

- Allowing the focus to drift into other areas that were not defined by the institution's mission statement.

Help your curriculum by making sure the students, parents, faculty, administrators, and all other stakeholders understand what it is designed to do. In other words, they must understand what results the curriculum is attempting to produce. This makes the institution more transparent while trying to please all of the stakeholders. Your learning outcomes should be clearly defined before your teach, or even plan, your lesson. This way, you can use your knowledge of what you want your students to learn to guide you through the lesson-planning process. The following is a sample of learning outcomes defined for a beginning college algebra class:

- After attending this class in MAC1101, Basic College Algebra, all students will be solving equations on their own to the degree of at least a 3 on a 5-point scale.

- After attending this class in MAC1101, Basic College Algebra, all students will understand how to follow the order of operations.

  + Acceptable evidence will include consistent demonstration of the ability to work the problem out, with the student's work shown below each problem.

- After attending this class in MAC1101, Basic College Algebra, all students will understand how to effectively write a mathematical equation from a word problem.

  + Students will be able to demonstrate this effectively and correctly 3 out of 5 times.

- After attending this class in MAC1101, Basic College Algebra, all students will be able to check their work to make sure they got the right solution to the problem.

  + Acceptable evidence will include the ability to show the checking process after each problem is solved.

To gauge how effective you were in relaying your message or the outcomes you defined to your students, you will need to have your students fill out an assessment about the lesson and how it was taught. For more information about this, see *Chapter 12*.

Defining a Good Course

It is somewhat difficult to define what makes a good course. As a teacher, however, designing the course and teaching it is your primary role. As you gain experience, you will develop your own preferences for how this is done. To start, a traditional approach with a detailed, typed outline might be the best way to organize your course. As you gain experience, you might design a course by making random notes on your computer or on pieces of scrap paper.

Here are some points to consider for defining a good course:

- Does the course challenge students to begin thinking in ways that involve solving problems, making decisions, and using creative and critical thinking? All courses require basic learning skills, such as comprehending and memorizing information.

- Students should receive immediate and frequent feedback on their learning. This means letting students know if they are grasping the material. It also means giving students daily or weekly feedback in a timely manner.

- Are you using active learning that requires students to solve problems and think critically? There will also be passive learning, such as listening and reading.

- Use a logical and structured sequence of learning exercises. This is another recurring theme: Building upon students' prior knowledge and allowing them to learn in a variety of ways, including writing, asking questions, and participating in discussion groups.

- Use fair assessments and grading practices. Design a grading system that is objective and based on what you have taught your students. It also helps to communicate it in writing.

Student Assignments

Most assignments you give will involve making presentations, solving problems, and writing papers. As you develop assignments, a key thing to keep in mind is how they allow your students to use or display their knowledge. Displaying knowledge involves presenting a text or visual assignment.

Another point to consider is that assignments can be formal or informal. A formal presentation, for example, would be prepared for the entire class using PowerPoint or other media. An example of an informal presentation would be role-playing in small groups. The same applies to writing assignments. Formal writing assignments involve term papers or essays. Informal writing involves note-taking or journaling.

When working with numbers, a formal presentation would be preparing graphs or charts. An informal assignment would be giving homework or having students work in groups. It is good to have a variety of assignments to offer students the chance to explore different learning techniques and to keep everyone interested. Within all assignments, strive to create ways students can build on the knowledge they have gained in prior assignments. Repetition is also helpful in making the information "stick."

Since you are creating all of the assignments for your course, you must be extremely organized. Being organized allows you to maximize the amount of time you have to teach during your class. If you know what is on your agenda for each class, and know precisely what you are going to say, you will not have to waste time during the lecture trying to think of what comes next. It pays to first look at your calendar and what you are planning to cover. Your plan might change over the weeks of your course, but penciling in a road map will give you a sense of structure and confidence.

For example, organizing the collection of student assignments can save a lot of time. If your students are going to be writing a lot of papers, set up folders and assign each one with a letter of the alphabet. When students enter your class, they can place their assignments in the folders according to their last name.

The folders can also be used for returning papers to students. But, you must respect student rights under the Family Educational and Rights Privacy Act (FERPA), which states that student grades are private. To get around this problem, you might post grades on an Internet-based system that requires students to log in to see their grades. You can also place the grade inside the pages and then staple the paper shut so that other students cannot see it.

It is worth mentioning here the importance of record keeping for assignments. Record everything as soon as possible in an organized fashion. Going back later on and trying to record everything will not only take more time, it can lead to errors.

Beginning Teaching and Ending a Lesson

Magic happens when a great teacher steps in front of a classroom. Doors to knowledge are unlocked and there are many "Aha!" moments as students learn from you and from each other. There is an exchange of information that is challenging and entertaining. Like magic, exactly how it happens can be difficult to define. Everyone has an opinion of what makes a lesson fantastic or boring. You no doubt have had teachers who were great examples of both. No one intentionally sets out to be dull or uninformative. You will spend a lot of time developing a teaching style and learning how to be a dynamic teacher. There are no magic formulas. Or are there? You might be surprised to learn that there is a method used by all kinds of public speakers, including preachers and politicians. Here it is:

1. Tell the audience (your students) what they are going to hear.

2. Present the information.

3. Close by reiterating what you told them.

The information that is put into this formula is what makes it unique for teachers. Everyone who gives a speech is trying to educate their audience, or at least put a spin on what they want the audience to know. Outside the classroom, if the audience misses the message there is no consequence in terms of a grade, unlike in the classroom when a student's grade can suffer because of misunderstanding a message or lesson. When politicians give a speech, no one in the audience is going to use that information to complete assignments or study for a test. In the classroom, the information you impart provides a foundation for what your students learn. It has direct impact on what grades they will receive, their academic standings, and ultimately their futures. Failing to pay attention to a politician's speech can have a negative effect on your future, but there is a distinct difference here. You are not trying to spin the information you are presenting for your own gain. You are offering information so students have a deeper understanding of the topic you are teaching.

When it comes to teaching, the basic formula for giving a speech can be modified to include the following:

- Presenting the information

- Allowing students to apply the information

- Asking students to use the knowledge in hands-on learning exercises

Added to this list are several ways to present the information. Among them are:

- Showing multimedia presentations

- Lecturing or telling students information

- Reading textbooks, online text, or other materials

- Demonstrations (how to weave a basket for a course in Basket Weaving 101)

- Field trips (going to the museum to see the King Tut exhibit)

- Observations (chronicling the lives of earth worms)

Ideas For Lessons

It is almost time for you to take the stage. You will not be passing out political buttons or receiving a standing ovation from your constituents, but you will be stepping into a spotlight just the same. Here you are, with a blinding light beaming down on your face. Now what? Please do not say you have forgotten your lines. The first few minutes are critical to grabbing your students' attention. This is when you tell them what you are going to teach and what you want them to learn. No one is calling it easy, but you must get your students' interest, consider their existing knowledge, and make the lesson relate to your students' lives. Experts say you have about 30 seconds to draw in your students or you leave them in daydream mode. Here are some ways to get them focused:

- Ask your students to challenge their thinking by making a provocative statement. ("I think martial law is a great idea because there is not enough discipline in this world and more people deserve to be in prison.")

- Use the latest campus, local, or national news and relate it to your topic. ("Today, more money was given to bail out the nation's financial institutions. How does this issue relate to the economic lesson we learned yesterday?")

- Ask students what they would choose if they only had two undesirable choices for solving a problem. (Would you rather rob a bank or go without food if you had no money?")

- Ask students to respond to a question that relates to the lesson. ("You are running for state senator and someone asks you if more funding will be available for state colleges. How do you answer them?")

Students start thinking when you open with a question. Hopefully their minds wake up and they start anticipating what they are going to learn. Then they are ready to go on a learning journey. Earlier in this chapter, you learned the importance of asking questions. You know that your students' existing knowledge will carry into every new lesson. Be aware that it will also influence their interpretation and understanding of what you are about to teach. You can assess what your students know by asking them to come up with a couple of questions about the topic you are going to teach. This is just one way to help you understand what they already know. It also gives them a stake in finding the answers to their questions. Another technique involves asking students to predict what will happen next. Questioning is just one of many tools you can use from your teaching arsenal.

Organizing your lessons can keep you on track and help you make sure that what your students are learning is relevant and worthwhile. Lessons and the course itself must be well-planned. An instructor must build upon more basic topics and lessons before graduating to the more complex. It will be hard for your students to learn if you jump from one topic to another, and then back to the first paragraph. Proper organization will help ensure that students do not miss an important topic and will hopefully keep them interested in lessons.

Remember being a student and asking yourself, "Why do I need to learn this?" Or, "Why is this important?" Making lessons relevant to students' lives is no less important today. Pointing out events from pop culture can help relate the information to students' lives. By doing this, you are making the lesson more interesting, and you are making it easier for students to remember because it relates to them. Making these kinds of connections only takes a couple of minutes, but it can make a big impact on how much students learn. Now let us look at another technique you can use in your classroom to break up lecturing time and make it a little more interesting.

Acting Out

Many studies point to hands-on learning as one of the most powerful learning tools because it helps students remember more. Hands-on learning is simply learning by doing. You cannot learn to drive a car in a classroom, for example. At some point, you must hit the road and drive the car.

Hands-on learning is not a new concept. It ties in to a philosophy that the more senses used when learning (sight, touch, sound, taste, and smell), the more likely you are to retain the information. Asking the students to make a PowerPoint presentation that uses pictures, text, and charts is one example of a hands-on learning activity involving technology. Normally, acting out in class has a negative connotation, but role-playing allows students to simulate scenarios and can introduce hands-on learning.

Using role-playing is just one of a variety of teaching techniques that help keep students interested. They come to class never sure of what to expect. For example, in a business class during a unit on the stock market, have your students come to class every day dressed in business attire. Then you can create the stock market atmosphere in your classroom as students act as day traders and investors in a mock stock market. This might sound unconventional for a college class, but your students will have a better idea about how the stock market works because of your innovative ideas. Never be afraid to think outside of the box.

The Perfect Ending

Every lesson needs closure. This is a time to summarize and tell students the key information they have learned, or let students discuss their new perceptions with each other. If you began the class with a question, review the answer to the question. Then, begin setting up for the next lesson ("Tomorrow, King Kong will make a guest appearance as we study the architecture of the Empire State Building"). If it was a particularly information-packed day, thank the students for their hard work.

Teaching Skills Employers Want

There is one more element you should consider when designing lessons: What skills are employers seeking? The goal in any education program is to make your students as employable as possible. This can come through teaching students good work habits, such as completing their work on time and always putting forth their best effort. It can also come in the form of technical skills. Technical skills are among those that can vary the most. Virtually every year, updates are made to popular computer graphic design programs such as Photoshop and Dreamweaver (a Web design program). However, there are basic business skills that never go out of style. Speaking before a large group without dying of stage fright, writing a killer business letter, effective time management, and working as part of a team are just a few skills that are highly valued in many industries. By giving your students the chance to practice some of these skills through your course, you will strengthen your lessons and give your students an advantage in the highly competitive job market.

TEACHER'S
TIP:

If possible, include information in your course about the skills employers want. This can make your students more employable after they graduate.

Here is a listing of some of the skills employers value:

Public speaking

Having your students give presentations in front of the class will make them more comfortable with public speaking. Many students avoid making presentations out of fear. But in the business world, being able to speak to small groups and a packed auditorium is a coveted skill. If you cannot incorporate presentations into your classroom, encourage students to ask questions or participate in discussions.

Writing

Writing well will give your students the ability to communicate professionally and effectively in business. Aside from being able to write papers, students should be able to edit, rewrite, and proofread. If relevant, have your students write in class, in addition to the papers and reports that are required. If you are an English teacher, encourage students to take more than English 101. Taking advanced writing courses will help them in college and in the workplace.

Teamwork

It often seems easier to work on a project alone. There are no people who talk too much, people who do not do their work, or people who are just difficult. Tell your students not to be discouraged by these common problems. Group activities are designed to help students learn more than what one person can do on his or her own. Encourage students to volunteer to be group or team leaders, for example. In the workforce, employers often have employees work in teams. Students who can demonstrate that they have had this experience will find favor with employers.

Multitasking and time management

The best college students are masters of the art of multitasking and time management. Organizing and managing schedules, free time, and course workloads are valuable skills. Employers value people who can multitask, prioritize work, and juggle many projects at once. Remind your students that procrastination will prevent them from developing these skills. Doing work at the last minute leads to poor quality at best. At worst, the work simply does not get done.

Planning

Daily planners are a student's best friend. As a college student, they must learn to organize and manage everything from exams to papers. The same is true in the workplace. Deadlines are less likely to be missed when employees have a plan for organizing their work. Learning to do this in college can be easily transferred into the workplace. It helps to teach students that work must be done professionally and on time.

Research

All of those dreaded research papers and projects really do have value in the workplace. Employers need employees who can investigate, seek different viewpoints, and identify important issues. When students learn how to gather information, analyze it, and apply what they have learned, they have gained a skill employers value.

Determination

A student who graduates summa cum laude, with dozens of ribbons and tassels decorating his cap and gown, is not always the best employee. A student who works every night at Burger King and is a single parent knows the importance of never giving up. She has the ability to achieve goals and overcome obstacles. Students can use this to their advantage in a job interview. So can students who took the most difficult classes and volunteered for projects that no one else would attempt.

Good grades

Students with good grades demonstrate to an employer that they have a good work ethic. Employers perceive students with good grades as being ambitious and productive. Employers believe (or hope) that a strong work ethic will transfer into the work environment.

Next, we will look more in-depth at the backbone of all classroom activities: The lecture. As mentioned earlier, it is important to assess what your students already know. This will help you design lectures that are neither too easy nor too complex for your students' knowledge level.

Chapter 8

The Art of Lecturing

Studies have long shown that lecturing is an ineffective form of teaching. So, why are so many teachers still doing it? Lecturing is the most common form of instruction at major colleges, especially in classes teeming with hundreds of students. The problem with lecturing is that it is a passive form of learning that fails to hold the interest of every student. Teachers that rely heavily on lecturing are simply carrying on the tradition of how they were taught. Besides, something has to be done to take up class time.

In all seriousness, lecturing is far more than standing in front of a group of students and reciting a speech. It involves the art of movement, facial expression, eye contact, voice, and gesture. All of these things can either enhance or detract from your lecture. You do not want to bore or annoy people. Most importantly, you want your students to retain as much information as possible. Studies show that in the first ten minutes of a lecture, students retain about 70 percent of the information. In the final ten minutes of a lecture, the retention rate drops to about 20 percent. These statistics might make you wonder if it is worth it to lecture at all.

TEACHER'S TIP:

Use a variety of lecturing methods to hold your students' attention for the duration of your class.

Of course it is worth it, because there are advantages. For example, lectures allow you to give your students the most up-to-date information available. Lectures are a good tool to summarize information from many different sources. Lectures are also more flexible than text. You can change the wording and material based on the knowledge level of your students. Although trade publications and technical journals can contain valuable information, their articles might be beyond your students' comprehension.

In addition to the lecture itself, consider if you need to give students a list of additional reading or other information. Handouts might be used, and should be carefully chosen. Make sure they support the information you gave during the lecture. They should be a tool students can refer to, so try to keep their use in line with the organization of your lecture. Another idea is making a list of facts, quotes, or complex issues. These can be handed out at the end of each section within your course or before tests. You can also post these materials to your course Web site, if you have one. All these materials will help you increase the effectiveness of your lesson.

CASE STUDY: HOW TO BE A SUPERSTAR LECTURER

Lorrie Houchin Thomas
Web marketing, social media market-
ing, and search engine marketing
University of California, Berkeley;
University of California, Santa
Barbara extension; Santa Barbara
City College

As a public speaker by profession, Lorrie Houchin Thomas has an advantage when it comes to lecturing. High-level speaking skills are required if one wants to be a great lecturer, she said. She advises teachers to go to Toastmasters or similar groups to practice and improve their speaking skills so they are comfortable getting up in front of a class.

But, the instructor is careful to point out that lecturing is more than talent at speaking in public. "It is about being prepared, really loving what you do, and using technology in the classroom," she said. Slideshows are the backbone of a lecture, Houchin Thomas said. A PowerPoint can be an effective and entertaining tool, if used correctly. Slideshows should include images, not just gobs of text.

Houchin Thomas considers herself a facilitator. She interacts with students and encourages critical thinking. In order to do that, she has to use imagery. In the era of YouTube and Facebook, lecturers must be entertaining — but professors need to find, and be comfortable with, their own unique style.

"It is about being entertaining, but it is also about taking what I need to get across and getting it delivered. You have also got to make it interactive," she said.

Houchin Thomas offered the following tips for creating great lectures:

1. Be passionate about your subject, and be energetic. If you are not that excited about it, your students will know immediately. I have always been passionate about teaching. I love teaching, and I love feeling organized and keeping the content new. I have seen professors that regurgitate the same content. It is really not the easy way to do it. I think

it makes lecturing much more difficult and you are not doing it with a lot of passion.

2. Be prepared. Slides and PowerPoints are really just a supplement to help keep things going. They simply facilitate whatever it is you are trying to cover in a particular lecture.

3. Be entertaining. Teaching today can be so media-driven. You have to make it entertaining, but you also want to make sure it relates to your core curriculum. Get creative in using applications that students like. I teach with Facebook. I have students post materials on the Web site and I post course materials on the Web site.

4. Ask for help. It is fine to ask for outside help with all of this. I have paid graphic artists to create the right visuals. I am not a graphics expert, but I have become a lot better at it. Graphics can really add a lot to your presentation. One of my favorite ways to start a Web marketing class is to show a picture of a dog jumping up and down and say, "I am just so excited about Web marketing."

5. Adapt lectures to your subject. Recognize that different subjects require different lecturing techniques. Even if you are teaching mathematics, do not be afraid of going outside the confines of traditional lectures. For example, you could use a PowerPoint presentation to highlight key notes. If you have 20 slides of algebraic equations, the students could print them out and have the notes next to them.

6. Project a professional image. When I started teaching, I was in my late 20s. I overdressed. I wore suits and I really projected a professional image to gain the trust of the students.

7. Be a storyteller. If I am using case studies, and I am showing real examples, I am doing a little bit of storytelling. In one of my social media marketing classes, I used Facebook and Twitter to show examples of a major tax negotiation between CPAs and the IRS.

8. Make a strong ending. When it comes to wrapping up a lecture, I like to start with a clear summary, then I say what the homework is and what we will be covering next week. Preparation is really the key. If you are prepared, it radiates throughout your whole lecture.

It might help to rehearse part of the lesson with a colleague, or even a student. A colleague — another expert in the field — might be able to understand your presentation. Your students might not. For this reason, it is a good idea to also run your lesson past a student. He or she will be able to alert you to jargon and other problems that can cloud what you are trying to say.

Your own expertise and enthusiasm for your topic can really shine during a lecture, inspiring your students to want to learn more. If done correctly, lecturing can help you become a better teacher. Lecturing is a presentation that forces you to organize your thoughts and key points to fit into a structured period of time. In many ways, lecturing can preserve the human element to learning that Web sites and e-mail fail to fully duplicate. There is much more opportunity for interaction. The elements of a good lecture include:

- An opening statement or summary

- An emphasis on key points

- Using real-life examples to illustrate points

- Using analogies

- Visual presentations that back up the information

Planning Lectures

It is important to plan your lectures to make sure they cover all of these areas. To do this, consider your topic, objective, and how it will be delivered. You should also prepare notes as a guide to accompany your lecture. As you already learned, it is important to use different techniques for every lecture, if possible, to help keep students interested. Lectures can be broken down into three areas: an introduction, delivery of the information, and a summary of the information.

A good introduction to the lecture is essential as it grabs the students' interest. After an interesting introduction, you can transition into the core of the information you want students to learn. Again, use discussions and other activities to make the lecture interactive. The final part of the lecture, the summary, is a recap of the most important information you covered.

It is also important to consider when a lecture should be used. Lectures are great for giving information to large audiences, presenting new information before a media presentation, offering a topic overview, or piquing student interest in a topic. Lectures are considered inappropriate for complex or abstract information, topics that require extended discussions, such as opinions or attitudes, and situations where students must synthesize or evaluate information. If you have decided a lecture is the only way to go, there are some things you can do to make sure it is the best it can be.

Effective lectures are interactive and provide a lot of communication between student and teacher, encourage questions, include problem-solving activities in small groups, use a variety of multimedia, and require limited note taking because students are provided copies of lecture notes. Effective lectures are not just about talking; they allow students to connect with each other and with their teacher.

Ineffective lectures have limited interaction between teacher and student, involve the teacher talking most of the time, allow for few or no questions, keep the student dependent on the teacher for the information, have no student activities or supporting media, and require students to take extensive notes. To avoid ineffective lectures, look at including interactivity in your lessons. Using media, for example, seems to be one of the biggest trends and one of the most popular ways to keep students interested.

Using media in lectures

Using media and other visual aids are important for keeping a lecture rolling. Many people learn better through pictures than through words. Keep in mind that these materials play a supporting, not starring, role. There are some common gaffes you can avoid when using visual presentations, especially if you are inexperienced in using them. One of the most common mistakes is standing so that your head is projected on the screen. Another problem is talking at the slides. Face your students as much as possible to keep them engaged in what you are saying.

TEACHER'S TIP:

Use social media in your lectures to show trending topics about what you are teaching about. Twitter, **http://twitter.com**, can help your students sound off on different topics and can aid discussion.

The PowerPoint presentation might be a great way to gain your students' attention, but your actual presentation still makes a big difference. It is tempting to read slides word for word. You already know your students can read. Allow your students a moment to read the information after it appears. After you highlight the information, give another brief pause so that your students have a chance to reflect on the information they just read.

Logistics

Ironing out the logistics of a lecture is a fairly easy process. You must consider how long your lecture will take. A good standard is a total of 45 minutes, with the last 15 minutes open for discussion and questions. You should also consider the number of students receiving the lecture. Interaction will be more limited in a lecture hall of 300 students than it will be with a circle of 20 students. Therefore, the shape and size of a lecture room also comes into play. Move students as you see fit to encourage easy inter-action. If your class is held in a large lecture hall, but your students only fill a third of the seats, ask those in the back to move forward to eliminate the gaps.

Making lecture notes

As a new teacher, do not make the mistake of trying to memorize your lec-ture. Even experienced teachers find this difficult to do. If you forget a sec-tion, you waste time trying to remember what you were going to say, and you will lose the attention of your students. Lecture notes keep you focused on the presentation instead of the next point you are going to make. They provide reminders such as phrases and key words in an outline format that you can look at while giving your lecture. You can keep your lecture notes on PowerPoint presentations, note cards, or regular paper.

By planning in advance, you can focus on making your lecture as dynamic and exciting as possible. When designing your notes, plan carefully and use good cues. Make small notations about the times you plan to start media presentations, change lighting, or make other visual changes. It is also good practice to use any visual aids before giving the lecture to ensure they work.

Lecturing with 'clickers'

In a classroom of 30 students, it is easy to gauge attentiveness because you can see your students' facial expressions. It becomes apparent who is listening, participating, and grasping the material. Lecturing a class of 100 students — or several hundred — is another story. Getting feedback and having students answer questions becomes an obstacle.

Some teachers are turning to clickers, a popular device used by audiences that watch and rate movies. Clickers, sometimes called classroom response systems, are similar to remote controls in size and function. The device allows students to send their answers to a computer, which displays the results anonymously on a projection screen at the front of the class. Clickers can be used for a single question or for opinion polls and quizzes. The results are displayed in bar graphs on a projection monitor at the front of the class. You might even decide to use the device to give students participation points.

With clickers, teachers can get answers from any amount of students in a matter of minutes. When the answers are totaled, it is instantly clear if the majority of the class is grasping the material or not. If students seem to be having trouble understanding that part of the lecture, you can go back and rephrase the material or initiate a class discussion.

Another advantage of using the clickers is student incentive to pay attention. Even though the program does not display the names of students with the answers, the teacher is able to see who gave what answers. A study at Ohio State University showed that college teachers often use clicker questions for about 20 percent of their class time. The rest of the time is spent on traditional discussions or lectures. Student participation with the clickers is about 90 percent. Students are not forced to answer the questions, but offering extra credit for answering can boost participation rates to nearly 100 percent. Participation also helps you keep track of student attendance. The Ohio State University study also showed that physics students who used clickers scored about ten percentage points higher on final exam multiple-choice questions than those who did not use clickers. That is the equivalent of one letter grade higher.

Clickers cost about $30 each and students can usually purchase them at the college bookstore. Some campuses provide the clickers, but do not require students to buy them. Different textbook publishers make different versions of clickers, so students could have to purchase multiple devices for different classes if the college does not set a standard.

Teaching Large Lecture Courses

A sizeable portion of the work involved in teaching a large lecture course takes place well before the first day of class. For example, it is easier in a small group to make a spur-of-the-moment assignment, but in large classes you might need to distribute written guidelines. You simply might not have enough time to explain it all and make sure everyone understood it. Similarly, in small classes, students can easily turn in their assignments during class. In large lectures, you must decide how to distribute and collect papers without consuming precious class time. All these tasks take planning and organization. Although the following tips are designed specifically to address the dynamics of a large class, you can apply many of them to small classes as well.

1. **Know your stuff.** Study the topic and try to anticipate student questions. Review some of the assignments, reading lists, and course materials used by others at the college who have taught your course. If there is a teacher in your department who is known for his or her electrifying lectures, ask if you can sit in on one of their classes.

2. **Do not talk too much.** No one wants to hear you talk for an entire class. Remember, the average student has an attention span that ranges from 10 to 20 minutes. After that, the retention rate drops. Break up the lecture with media, small groups, or a demonstration.

3. **Vary the information.** Include complex analyses, controversial issues, and varying points of view to keep student interest. This also helps develop their thinking skills.

4. **Watch the clock.** You do not want the lecture to end too early. Also, make sure you allow class time for quizzes, exams, and other activities. Cramming all the necessary information in between these other activities can be a challenge.

5. **Know your audience.** Your approach will be different for an 8 a.m. group of freshmen than it will be for a group of seniors graduating in a couple of months. In other words, consider the material along with your students' ability level. This will also help guide you regarding how much information you should cover, how much review you should do, and how much detail to include.

6. **Write down the topic and why it is important.** Come up with the single most important thing you want your students to remember. Do not overload them with a lot of figures and other details they probably will not remember. Focus on a few key points.

7. **Present the material in a logical fashion.** Some lectures were born to be chronological. Others were not. Depending on your topic, you might choose to go from a general overview into more specific points. You might introduce a problem, and then offer a solution. Yet another technique is to offer a statement, and then prove or disprove it.

8. **Block your lectures.** Think of your lecture as a presentation broken in to several 15 minute segments (or whatever time frame you choose). Each section should include transition points and a summary before you move on to the next point. Make a note of some areas that can be cut or reduced if you start running out of time. Do not forget to begin and end your lecture with a summary of key points. This gives you a chance to mention what will be coming in the next lecture.

9. **Use anecdotes and examples.** Examples that are visual or create a picture in the mind's eye can make your points more

memorable. Some teachers recommend having more examples than you think you might need. That way, you have an arsenal that can help you better explain the information to your students.

10. **Choose your words wisely.** Using unclear words or sentences can cause confusion for your students. It is best to use short, easy words that will not have your students reaching for their dictionaries. Use introductory phrases that alert your students to transitions. For example, "Now we can move on to..." Or, "Another point of view is..."

11. **Allow time for questions.** This can be done before, during, or after the lecture. Planning for questions allows you to better manage your time (and your students' time).

CASE STUDY: A STUDENT-CENTERED APPROACH

Timothy Caldwell
Director of choral activities,
instructor of voice
University of Maine

Lectures have never been a part of voice instructor Timothy Caldwell's lessons. As the Director of Choral Activities at the University of Maine in Orono, Caldwell has always taken a non-traditional, student-centered approach to his teaching.

Although he said his skills and strategies are worlds apart from where he began in his first year teaching college, Caldwell has always believed that the most important aspect of any classroom is creating an awareness in the students, a belief that has evolved since he began teaching college in 1972.

"University professors are not taught how to teach," he said. "We are hired based on our degrees and professional experience within our fields of study. " So, Caldwell began teaching college following in the footsteps of how he was taught while he was in college, implementing the same teaching methods in his classes about techniques for the singing actor, and other music/theater classes.

Based on results of neurological studies and the findings of educational psychologists, Caldwell operates his classroom under the belief that when students are actively involved in learning, they learn and retain more because they are engaging their emotions in the process. To really connect with his students, Caldwell uses an outcome-based syllabus, in which goals are made for the course. For example, the syllabus will include things such as, "By the end of the semester, you are expected to demonstrate the following…" Thus, the material is taught differently than in a traditional course, where the syllabus is broken down by what content will be taught when.

"I never lectured," he said. "All the classes I taught have been performance classes or skill-development, so students were always active in the classes." And with an approach like this, the sky is the limit for effectively implementing material into the course, he said.

Relaxing Before a Lecture

The very first lecture you give will probably be nerve rattling. If you are a person who tends to let your imagination get the best of you, try using some relaxation tips to ease anxiety. Learning to relax is easy for some teachers and difficult for others. You want to be alert and energetic, but not too keyed up. Here are some tips that can help make you more comfortable:

- Eat a light meal before your lecture. Eating a heavy meal will make you lethargic; you want to be able to move around the room for dramatic effect.

- Take a brief walk to energize yourself and burn off any excess energy. Or, find your own way of relaxing before giving a lecture.

- Arrive early. Make sure all of your materials are in place, and that all equipment is working properly. Also, look over your notes briefly.

- Ensure that your lecture includes smooth transitions from one point to the next.

- Make sure the lighting and room temperature (if possible) are at comfortable levels.

- Have a bottle of water available during your lecture.

- Take a few deep breaths before starting.

Defining a Good Lecture

It is easy to list the elements of a good lecture, but it is more difficult to measure them. Some questions to ask yourself are whether the students enjoyed the lecture, how effectively you conveyed information, how much of an impact you made on the students, and how you can improve the lecture. Other ways to evaluate your lectures include asking for student feedback, having a colleague or administrator watch you, and conducting a self-evaluation.

One of the best tools for improving your lecture technique is also one of the most painful: videotaping yourself. This gives you the most accurate view of how your lecture sounded and whether you covered every key point you set out to make. The videotape will tell you for certain if you droned on in a monotone voice for 50 minutes. Again, it might be helpful to have a colleague watch the video and offer you some praise and criticism. Watching yourself on tape might also bring to light some positive (or negative) things that you were not even aware of doing. Are you pulling at your collar repeatedly, or not making enough eye contact with your students? After watching the video, make a list of the areas you need to improve.

Chapter 9

Great Debates

People love to talk. Whether it is a presidential race or a basketball game, people like to weigh in when things happen. They do it by blogging, sending e-mails, or talking with family or friends. The same concept applies to lecturing. You "make news" in the classroom by talking or giving assignments, and your students discuss it. Discussions give students the chance to critique, interpret, and ask questions about the information being presented. Hopefully, it will all lead to deeper thinking about your subject.

It is to be expected that emotions flare over controversial issues. The topics you teach might touch upon students' religious, political, or personal beliefs and values. This can create strong reactions. These hot-button topics include abortion, illegal immigration, discrimination, civil liberties, and evolution. Emotions can also be released with issues such as serious illnesses, bankruptcy, drug abuse, or the suicide of a friend or family member, especially if a student has experienced one of these events in their lives. This is not to say that controversy should be avoided. Difficult discussions will no doubt arise outside of the classroom. Tell your students that exploring emotional topics inside the classroom will better equip them to discuss these topics outside of the classroom. Assure them that emotional reactions are normal and inevitable when talking about issues that have impacted their lives. When discussing touchy subjects, it is best to steer the discussions so they are based on facts or research. Introducing personal opinions can lead to personal attacks. If a heated discussion breaks out, have students summarize what others are saying before they make a statement. It helps maintain neutrality.

TEACHER'S TIP:

Be sure to establish rules before beginning a debate so things do not get too heated.

There will have to be some decorum to ensure that learning happens and students do not feel threatened during discussions. As a teacher, it is up to you to make your classroom a safe place. This means that it is all right for students to agree to disagree. Let them know this can be done without swearing, being condescending, or insulting classmates. Showing a little respect can go a long way. On the other hand, it is important for students to not become insulted or hurt if others disagree with their opinions or question what they are saying.

Creating a "safe" classroom means setting some ground rules. Do not feel you must take on this task all alone. Ask your students to help you establish some discussion guidelines. By now, college students have likely been in other classroom discussions, even if it was only in high school. They already know what makes a good discussion group or a bad one. With this in mind, set your students on a course for their first discussion: What makes a good discussion? Ask students to talk about the positive and negative experiences they have had in past discussion groups. In good ones, there are a lot of robust interactions, people are enthusiastic, and you walk away feeling refreshed, as if you learned something. Bad discussion groups are filled with bullies that yell or swear and interrupt others when they are talking. They make other people feel intimidated. Shy students might stop talking if they are worried that they will be insulted or laughed at.

From this discussion, ask students to help create guidelines for how discussion groups will operate. Some suggestions you might make for your students include:

- Each student is required to participate in every discussion.

- What happens in the classroom stays in the classroom.

- Be respectful of everyone's opinion and allow everyone an opportunity to talk.

- Do not laugh at others unless they are trying to be funny.

- No personal attacks are allowed.

Group discussions are a good place for students to practice speaking in front of others. They allow them to consider new opinions, articulate their own opinions, and ask questions. Be sure to monitor student discussions. If they are breaking the discussion guidelines, step in and offer some advice to help them get back on track.

Preparing for a Discussion

The first thing to consider is whether your topic lends itself well to a discussion. As you plan your course, allot time for discussion groups throughout the semester. To make a discussion effective, allow students some time to prepare in advance. About a week prior, give them a list of questions to think about. Some of these can be drawn from the techniques that help students read a textbook. They include asking why the material is important, keeping track of the key points, and interpreting what it means. Do not worry about "giving away" the gist of the discussion by asking these questions. You want students to be well-prepared for the discussion to promote participation. The greater their depth of understanding about the topic, the easier it will be for them to debate with other students. Just as we saw with icebreakers and other activities, it can also be helpful to have students write down their answers. This helps them to remember, and it can be of particular help to quiet students who find it difficult to think off the top of their heads. If you use written questions, make sure you decide how to collect them, as well as whether or not students will receive grades or extra credit for their work.

CASE STUDY: THE PROS AND CONS OF USING STUDENT DISCUSSION GROUPS

Myrtle Freeman
Tarrant County College South Campus, Fort Worth, Texas

Myrtle Freeman uses discussion groups to help her students prepare for group debates. Each semester, her students debate major topics in government. After covering the U.S. Constitution, Freeman lectures on rights and liberties. She picks two current event issues — such as capital punishment and abortion — and splits the class into four groups with one pro and one con group for each topic.

The groups discuss their stance on an issue, with all students participating. "This requires them to do some critical thinking. For example, they might discuss what arguments there are in favor of the death penalty. This allows them to talk among themselves, and I am sitting there as a consultant. I can come in and say they should raise issues based on logical reasoning. I try to give them some ideas on how they would prioritize their arguments," Freeman said.

In consulting with the students, Freeman attempts to direct them down the path toward the strongest argument, along with some counter arguments related to their position on the issue. Freeman requires the students to develop about four to five major arguments and the same number of counterarguments to anticipate the points their opponents will raise.

In order to facilitate the discussion, Freeman hands out a worksheet which she asks students to work on together within their groups. The groups do statistical analyses, examine data on the Internet, and find answers to questions that come up during the discussion. Freeman requires her students to have statistics to back up their arguments, document their sources, write a group paper, and summarize their findings for class.

"I do not want them to say they do not agree with the death penalty because they think it is a bad thing," Freeman said. "I want them to express their opinions based on facts and research."

Freeman pointed out there will be differences in personalities among group members. Those who enjoy following current events might naturally dominate the discussions, while others do not say much. This is another reason instructors must remember to act as facilitators.

The goals of her debates and discussions are not only to teach some basic skills in independent research; she also wants to develop and enhance their social skills by allowing them to interact with each other. "College is really a microcosm of society and students are learning many skills. They are learning discipline, humility, working with others. Oftentimes, they will learn new things just from working with each other," Freeman said.

Directing the Discussion

Write down the questions you plan to use for your discussions ahead of time. This allows you to word the question as clearly as possible, and will keep you on track during class time. You might want to write the question on the board so students can reread it while they think of their replies. When you ask a question, allow a pause so that students can collect their thoughts. Allowing a few moments of dead air will take some discipline on your part. It is natural to want to keep talking. By allowing students a few moments to think, you will improve the answers you receive. You do not want students to worry about answering a question too quickly. Try to avoid using specific student names when asking a question to keep it fair game for everyone. Since many people are visual learners, a diagram projected on a screen is another good way to begin a discussion. If you are working with a large class and not small groups, be careful to make the session a discussion, not question-and-answer time. If you ask a question and one student responds, ask other students to respond to what was just stated.

Problem Areas

To speak or not to speak

Quiet students will need to be prodded to talk in class. If you have a widespread problem with students not participating, consider making the groups smaller. They might not feel as self-conscious talking in front of a smaller number of people. Another technique is to ask students for their opinions, so they are not as concerned about giving the wrong answer. You might have to work with the quiet ones a little bit more. Remember, it is important for students to have experience in holding formal discussions with others because they will be expected to do this in most workplaces.

Then there are students who ramble on, talk too much, or interject comments at inappropriate times. Aside from intimidating other students, they can intimidate new teachers. Try averting eye contact with the student when they talk, and they will probably get the message. It might be necessary to take the student aside outside of class and tactfully talk with them. Praise them for their enthusiasm, but explain that "not everybody is as able to express himself or herself so freely" and you would like everyone in the class to have an opportunity. Depending on how assertive the student is, you might consider asking them to limit the number of times they talk in class. You can also place the outspoken student in a role where they cannot talk as much. For example, have them make a written summary of all of the points being made in the discussion. You can format the discussions so that each student is required to talk. That makes it impossible for one person to monopolize the discussion. In some cases, students do not realize they are thwarting the discussion. All they need is some guidance from you. In other cases, a student might be deliberately cruel. These situations require an immediate intervention on your part.

Unintended humor

If a student laughs at another student's answer, it is important to diffuse the situation right away. Do not let a student undermine one of their peers or your authority in the classroom. If you fail to correct this, other students might think they will be laughed at, too. If this happens, you can say something such as, "Now let's consider this for a minute. When might this viewpoint apply?"

You are not immune to being laughed at, either. Some unintended slapstick is bound to happen: A door knob falls off when you grab it, the PowerPoint is so tiny no one can read it, the projection screen unexpectedly rolls up during a presentation — you get the idea. Do not ignore it, because that only increases the awkwardness of the situation. It also makes it appear as if you really are embarrassed. Acknowledge the blooper and move on. ("Oh well, so much for opening the door to knowledge." "Did anyone bring a magnifying glass?" "Well, I really was not finished with that.") There is nothing wrong with showing you are not infallible and that you have a sense of humor. These things can actually make you more likable, as long as your class is not in a constant state of equipment malfunctions.

Stalled Discussions

Discussions might fall flat, despite your best planning efforts. If this happens, you can troubleshoot some of the potential causes. Ask students if the reading material was too boring or maybe a little over their heads. Are you making everyone feel as if his or her contributions are valued? Get your students to make some written responses if you are not sure. You could have students write down why they are not participating in the discussions or why they think they are not running smoothly. The best approach might be to ask students specific questions. These can include questions about the difficulty level of the material, their classmates, times they felt bored, or things they did not understand. You could even have a discussion about why discussions are not working. You might find that some of your students are simply shy about speaking up in class.

Going off-topic

Whether you should intervene in a discussion depends on how long it has gone off-topic. You want students to converse with each other and have a sense of camaraderie. However, you do not want them to waste 20 minutes talking about last night's football game. To get the discussion back on track, try to use whatever they are talking about and relate it back to the topic. In some cases, of course, this will be impossible. If that is the case, you can remind students what the topic is and give a little explanation about why this material will be important later on, especially if it will be graded or will appear on an exam. Finally, if the discussion is about a person, you can always ask the students to consider what that person would have said about whatever they are talking about that is off-topic. This might seem like a stretch, but asking what Sigmund Freud might say about a football game could lead to some pretty interesting responses.

Lack of preparation

It will be a nightmare for you and your students if they arrive to class unprepared for the discussion. How can you jump-start a discussion when no one knows what is being discussed? If you get a sense that this has happened, ask for a show of hands for everyone who completed the assignment to help them prepare.

TEACHER'S
TIP:

Have your students research current events related to your debate topic to help them understand the importance of the issue you are debating.

Assuming you get honest answers, this will let you know whether a discussion will be feasible. The best way to deal with this problem is to prevent it from happening. You can ask students to prepare one question to ask, or have them select a passage they would like to discuss. Alternatively, assign students to specific roles. Have one summarize their findings for the rest of the class, for example.

Discussion closed

At the close of the discussion, summarize what was discussed and recap some of the highlights. Show the students how the discussion helped them to learn more by allowing them to see viewpoints outside of their own. You can do this by discussing them and writing the information down on the screen. Also, tell students why the material was related to an assignment or test. Remind students that their participation is important because being able to discuss a topic shows they have a strong grasp of it. Also, do not forget to thank everyone for contributing. Make a special note for the quiet students who had a major breakthrough by actively participating in the discussions.

Chapter 10

Getting to Know Your Students

Behind every student's face is a story. As you look out at the faces of the students in your class, recognize that you have no idea where they have been. You have no idea about their lives, or even what happened the night before they arrived in your classroom for the first time. Mixed among your group of students are individuals with financial problems, emotional problems, dating problems, or even the self-imposed lack of discipline and time management. Then, there are the students that party all night and sleep late. They hand in sloppy work because they think they can get away with it. A story about saving starfish that have washed up on a beach is sometimes used by educators in relating how they help students succeed in their academic careers. The idea is that you can only save a few of the starfish. You cannot save all of them. In fact, some of the issues and problems your students have might impact or stop their college careers, if only temporarily.

Being a Teacher Versus a Friend

You might have chosen your career because of a desire to help students and make a difference. If you fall into this category, be careful to not burn yourself out by getting overly involved in your students' problems. You will naturally emanate a caring attitude if you fall into this category. Because of this, students will seek out your counsel if they are having problems. Compassion can prompt us to relate our own life experiences that were similar and tell how we pulled through it.

TEACHER'S **TIP:**

Guide students toward professional counseling services offered on campus if his or her problems are serious and merit professional counseling.

Your campus counseling center will have business cards or brochures that tell students how and when to contact them, and most services are free. Keep some of the cards and brochures in your office or briefcase. When students seek you out for advice, take time to listen with sincere concern. Then, tactfully pull out one of the cards and refer the student to counseling. You do not have the time to be a student's best friend or counselor, even though you might want to try to help. Referring students to a trained professional is the best help you can give. Remember that you can list counseling services on your course syllabus in the section that tells students about the various resources offered on campus. These can include suicide hotlines and resources for drug and alcohol abuse, crime victims, and other serious or emergency situations. You might not want to list all of these on your syllabus, but you should have the numbers readily available in case you need them.

Legal Issues

You should avoid getting too wrapped up in your students' lives. It might sound harsh, but you cannot afford to risk trying to save a student at the expense of your own emotional and financial wellbeing. You can still place yourself at risk even with the best of intentions. What if a student comes to you with concerns about committing suicide? You decide not to tell anyone and then it happens. During an investigation into the death, police learn that the student told her roommate she was talking to you about her problems. Naturally, the parents are in shock, and they go into a tailspin when they hear this. They need someone to blame, and they decide to launch a lawsuit against you.

Now you are in financial peril, as well as having to deal with your own feelings of guilt and remorse. The college decides to place you on leave until the final outcome of the lawsuit. Your contract might not be renewed the following year. Being a first-year teacher makes you particularly vulnerable to this kind of outcome. As tragic as the student's death is, another casualty has resulted. Your own career and reputation are now on life support. If you leave the campus under a shroud of controversy, finding another job can be difficult, especially in a tough economy. Any business or organization will be gun-shy about hiring someone even remotely associated with a lawsuit. You just might be a bungling goofball that could cost them a lot of money down the road.

Protect your reputation

Keep in mind that there are students who will have no problem causing you trouble, especially if it means saving their own academic hides. This can happen when a student is on the verge of failing your class. Then there are misunderstandings and rumors. A student might accuse you of making a romantic overture. If you listen to what the mainstream media says, romantic entanglements between teachers and students are common. That is why it is important to protect yourself from innuendo or accusations.

TEACHER'S TIP:

Do not shut the door entirely when students come to your office to meet with you.

Keep your door open at least a couple of inches when meeting with students. This reinforces the notion that the discussion is being held openly. It also establishes an air of professionalism, and helps keep the conversation geared toward academics.

When you meet with students, document the conversation by making notes on what you talked about. Be sure to include the date, time, and how long you met. Now you have a written record of what transpired. This does not mean that you are being paranoid. You are simply documenting what took place. It will also be helpful if the student meets with you again. You can easily refer to the record to refresh your memory about what you previously discussed.

Compassionate leadership

As a teacher, you must strike a balance between being compassionate and keeping the class on track. You will probably have no way to verify if what a student tells you is true or not. Problems that interfere with your students' academic progress can be isolated or chronic. You do not want to be too harsh, but you cannot be a doormat, either. If a good student comes to you with a problem, you can always do something, such as make a reasonable extension for completing an assignment. When an exception is made, remember to reinforce the requirements of your course and why it is important to complete everything on time. Difficult decisions might have to be made if the deadline for withdrawing from a class has passed and the student is in danger of failing. You certainly cannot pass a student who does not complete the work, no matter how awful their circumstances might be.

As a first-year teacher, though, it is best to use some caution when making a decision to pass or fail a student. An administrator can help you see the situation from an objective standpoint. Depending on the problem, the administrator might make special provisions to help the student complete the course work. Because you are new to teaching, you are not familiar with all of the options. Not only that, you will have someone who can back up the decision if questions come up later.

Finding a balance between being too compassionate and being too strict is not the only balancing act you will face as a first-year teacher. You must also develop some cultural sensitivity if you do not have it already. More and more minorities are enrolling on college campuses.

Accepting Diversity

Between 2000 and 2005, the most recent figures available, the percentage of black college students increased from 11.3 percent to 12.7 percent, while Hispanic students went up from 9.5 percent to 10.8 percent, according to the National Center for Education Statistics. As minority populations increase in our nation, it is only logical that the number of minority college students will continue to grow. Starting with the civil rights movement in the 1950s, opportunities for a college education began opening up for students of all ethnic and socioeconomic backgrounds. There has also been a movement to get more minorities involved in advanced high school courses so they have an equal opportunity at a college education.

Recognizing stereotypes

Ask yourself what stereotypes you hold about various groups. These can be socioeconomic, religious, ethnic, or even geographical in relation to the United States. In your mind, is one group of students going to be more driven than another? Are some of your students going to struggle with writing an English paper because of their background? Which students are going to be the top performers? Which will be the worst? Although we might not like to admit it, we all carry stereotypes in our minds. These stereotypes can come from things we heard growing up, statistics about how various student groups perform on SAT tests, graduation rates, and other categories. To help keep these stereotypes in check, it is important to remember that each student is an individual. Look at your language, as well. Make sure you are not using derogatory labels: Yankees, rednecks, or trailer trash. Gender is another stereotype to keep in check. Avoid making generalizations about males and females, and use both male and female pronouns when using examples in class. Here are some other ideas to help students feel more comfortable in your classroom:

- Do not allow students in your classroom to make slurs or jokes that show insensitivity. Let them know this behavior is unacceptable.

- Do not automatically appoint student spokespeople for various issues that concern their race or personal features.

- Recognize that some students might avoid eye contact and talking in class because it is considered disrespectful in their culture. Know that cultures have different definitions for "personal space."

- Students from other nations might need some assistance with English language skills. Look into what your campus offers for these students. Your campus might have special tutoring for students who speak English as a second language.

- Treat all students fairly and show no preferences for certain groups.

Learning more about diverse students

It is also helpful to show a genuine interest in your students' cultural backgrounds, especially if your class has a large specific minority group. At appropriate times, (after class or in the student union center) ask students to talk about their beliefs and traditions. You can also research various cultures by reading about them online or through articles and books.

Other ways to show an interest include attending student cultural groups, attending cultural celebrations, or contacting various campus and community organizations. By showing an interest in your students' differences, avoiding prejudicial language, and keeping your classroom free of racial slurs, you will make all students feel welcome. One of the characteristics of a good teacher is investing in one's students from an academic standpoint.

Be aware of your nonverbal communication, as well. Hand signals for example, carry different meanings in different cultures. Remember when President George Bush gave the "Hook 'em Horns" sign while overseas? The hand signal, with which involves raising just the pinky and index finger, represents school spirit at University of Texas at Austin, whose mascot is a longhorn cow. The hand signal takes on a completely different meaning in other parts of the world, like in Europe, where it signals a salute to Satan. This point illustrates how easy it can be to unintentionally offend another culture by using a hand signal.

TEACHER'S TIP:

Allow the information you learn about your students' cultures to shape some of the things you teach in class.

Instead of viewing all of this as walking across a cultural mine field, recognize that it can add depth to your classroom. For example, you could ask your students whether or not history teachings have presented a discriminatory view of American Indians. What about the scientific research or other findings done by minorities that did not receive due credit for their work? What were the important roles of women in the topics your students are studying?

Before you were interviewed for your teaching job, you researched your college and its demographics. This should give you a good idea of how much student diversity you will see in your class and which groups are most likely to be represented. Remember that, as a teacher, your goal is to help all students learn and feel welcome.

Chapter 11

What is Important to Students?

U p to this point, it might seem as if the emphasis has been on what your students want, and not so much what you want or expect from them. In many respects, these two issues go together. You cannot have one without the other. Teaching is a partnership, a learning adventure that you and your students are going on together. Your job as a teacher is to do more than impress students with your degrees and intellect. The goal is to use your talents to stretch your students into areas of learning they never knew existed.

Certainly, you will not be able to give your students everything they want. If they coast through an entire semester, you cannot give them an "A." On the other hand, there are some things you can do that your students will enjoy and will benefit you both. All of this does not have to be a mystery. If you want to know what your students are looking for from you and your class, ask them. You can do this by asking them to write down or e-mail you answers to a series of questions. This can be done in a matter of minutes. A few of the questions you might ask your students are what they expect from you, what they want to learn, some of the best and worst learning experiences they have ever had, and any other input they would like to give you. Do you have to try to please everyone? No, of course not. This exercise is simply a tool for you to use to modify your lessons or teaching style depending on the information you receive. A key theme here is to be responsive to your students.

CASE STUDY: BUILDING RAPPORT WITH STUDENTS

Moshe Davidow
Adjunct lecturer in services and marketing
Technion, Israel Institute of Technology

For Moshe Davidow, an adjunct lecturer at Technion, the Israel Institute of Technology, learning requires trust. "If my students do not trust me, then it compromises the entire process. Rapport is an important part of the trust process. Students need to know that I mean what I say and that I will be there for them. The students may be able to learn without rapport, but not as well. It is the difference between being forced to do something versus wanting to do it," Davidow said.

Davidow said if he takes an interest in his students, they reciprocate. He feels it critical to get to know as many students by name as possible. He does this by studying the photos attached to students forms. He tries to use their names in class and sees how many he gets right. If he is wrong, he finds out the right name and also who belongs to the other name. In large classes, he uses permanent seating and classroom maps to take attendance. He focuses on learning the names of students seated in certain sections each class.

"This usually works for large classes of up to 100 or so. I am not sure if it is feasible for classes of 300 to 400. There is a cost/benefit to learning all those names and, at some point, you realize that large intro courses might not be the best place to learn all students' names. Yet, I would at least focus on some of them," Davidow said.

Another method Davidow uses to build rapport is treating everyone with respect. He encourages his students to participate in classroom discussion and respect other students. He asks their opinions and tries not to embarrass them.

"I try not to take myself too seriously — as opposed to the course material,"Davidow said. "On the first day of class, I usually try to break the ice with something funny to say about myself or about my personal experience...Since they usually expect the professional stuff, it breaks the ice."

He includes personal stories throughout his course. "I do this by sharing with them my personal "war" stories, either as a manager or as a consumer. The examples relate to the course material and illuminate it. Using personal stories makes it more alive for the students."

Davidow acknowledges that it can be tricky to help students with their personal problems. He attempts to help students because he sees it as a way to show them he cares. If he feels a problem is too big for him to assist them, he directs them to someone who is able to help.

To make sure he is teaching in a manner most beneficial to his students, Davidow uses his student forms to question them about their hopes for a course. This allows him to address their expectations and make appropriate adjustments to the curriculum. If he feels he is missing rapport with his students, he provides them with a forum to express their concerns, and answers them by either making changes or explaining to them why no changes will be made. Either way, Davidow said, the very act of listening to their concerns can sometimes help if it is perceived as sincere.

Sometimes teachers can use rapport to make a lasting impression on students. Davidow is still in touch with some of his former students from 10 to 15 years ago. "They tell me how meaningful it was that I treated them with respect, knew their names, and took an interest in them. Some tell me about the class rules that made a positive impact on how they live," he said. "Some have told me that I showed them that it was acceptable to be different. I love hearing from them, and knowing that I made a difference."

Teaching with Personality

Surveys of college students show that being available, open, and respectful are some of the most important qualities a college teacher can have. Students say these qualities impact how well they learn a topic and how much of an impression the class has on them long after the semester is over. There are small ways you can give students these things. A lot of it has to do with sincerity, and not necessarily the amount of time you spend on a topic.

You do not have to turn your classroom into a comedy hour, but it does help to have a sense of humor. A little laughter is good, because it makes people relax. Students will have enough anxiety about whether they can learn everything in your class and complete every assignment. Laughter lightens the mood and can help open the door to learning. A sense of humor comes naturally to some teachers. Trying too hard to be funny when you really are not will still make students laugh, but not for the right reasons. If your timing is a little off, you can always use humorous quotes or appropriate cartoons in your PowerPoint presentations or on your Web site.

TEACHER'S TIP:

A sense of humor makes you seem more approachable, more than a headpiece yakking in front of the class and handing out assignments.

Students want to know how what they are learning relates to everyday life. They ask themselves, "Why are we learning this?" One way you can make these connections is to mention current events or popular movies and make a correlation to the topic at hand in your class. Another way to do this is to tell stories from your personal life that relate to the information you are teaching.

People who love their job are invigorating to be around. If you truly love teaching your subject, it will shine through. If a teacher is going through the motions just to get through the day, that also shows. Students want a teacher who loves what he or she is teaching. While no one can be perfect every day, a true love of what you do will help you rise above your off days.

You will not win any points for being overly sarcastic, disrespectful, or for embarrassing students. Doing any of these things might just land your name on a Web site where students rate their professors. While many of the ratings are favorable, others are not. The site **www.ratemyprofessor.com** boasts "6,000 schools, one million professors, and eight million opinions." The ratings section for a teacher shows the total number of ratings, the "easiness" of a class, average helpfulness, average clarity, and even a "hotness" total (just for fun).

If nothing else, Web sites like this shed some light on what is important to students. Students want a teacher who is helpful, enthusiastic about what they are teaching, presents the material in a clear fashion, sets clear and realistic expectations, and makes connections between the material and real life. This is surely something to consider in the way you treat your students. Yet, there is no reason to be fearful that a student will say something negative about the way you operate your class. It is probably going to happen more than once over the course of your career. The idea is to not give them excuses to issue complaints, whether on campus or online.

What else do students want? They want an environment that is positive: a place where they feel confident about expressing themselves without being ridiculed or attacked. Students also want prompt feedback from you on how they are doing. You can provide this during question-and-answer sessions in class.

Always have your grades accessible for your students. You will have many students who will constantly ask about their grades.

In earlier chapters, the importance of learning student names was mentioned. This is one of the key ways to help students feel as if they matter. If you do not even know their name, it is difficult to impart how important they are. By the same token, do not beat yourself up if you forget a name in a class of 250 students. More than likely, the student will understand if you "forget" their name in a class that size.

Then there are things that students might not forgive. Just like you, students want to feel they are getting the best value for their time and money. That leads to the question of whether or not students are customers. This is a loaded concept that will create a strong reaction for some teachers. You might want to think about it though, especially as a first-year teacher.

Students as Customers

Universities and colleges are not fast food restaurants where people can stroll through the door and demand to "have it their way." When an education is served up in college, the faculty and administrators design the menu. This includes how many classes are given, what they are, and the times they are held. The staff members are the experts, and they are the ones responsible for determining classes and college policies, but the needs of students should not be ignored.

In some ways, students are customers, and in other ways, they are not. In an educational setting, a lot of questioning takes place. Students are free to ask questions, agree or disagree with the viewpoint of their peers and teachers, and draw their own conclusions. For the most part, this behavior will not make you popular in the business world. Dissension is not often highly valued in corporate America. An argument can also be made that many colleges and universities receive state funding, federal or state grants, and are held accountable to the communities where they operate. There are exceptions, but it is generally not true of businesses. If a manufacturer decides to start making flying saucers instead of cars, the public has little, if any, say in it.

Keep in mind that the students' tuition pays a large portion of the education services they are buying. It is their money that allows the college to operate. If no one were enrolled in the college, there would be no classes to teach and no jobs for teachers. Similar to a business customer, a student can always go somewhere else if they are not satisfied. So, even though students do not own the college, they are still making an investment in it. Therefore, students might feel that the college should be more responsive to them in terms of the availability of courses, teacher's office hours, and the courses that are offered. Some colleges have student unions, which allow students to serve as advisors on various committees for this reason. They give students a chance for their voices to be heard.

Chapter 12

Assessing Students and Yourself

igher-education institutions require it, and teachers and students dread it. Grading student work, however, is a part of being a successful teacher. You have no choice but to evaluate your students' performance and to issue a verdict in the form of a letter grade. No one should underestimate the gravity of grading. Once a grade is issued, it leaves an indelible mark on a student's academic record. This is true of final grades and, of course, everything leading up to them. The grade you give each student has the potential to impact whether they make the dean's list, their acceptance into graduate school, or possibly their future employment.

TEACHER'S
TIP:

Always be mindful that your grades carry weight for your students' degrees and, ultimately, their futures.

You will likely fret at some point over the accuracy of the grades you levy upon students. Did a student really deserve an "A"? Was that "C" presentation really a "B" effort, instead? Grading is difficult and time-consuming, and it will be especially challenging for a new teacher. Familiarize yourself with the technical requirements for grading as outlined by your department. Depending on where you teach, you will have department guidelines to follow, deadlines for submitting grades, and requirements for reporting plagiarism or cheating. Be sure to follow all of these policies to a "T." The following grading scale is used by Dr. Marlene Caroselli (Chapter 13), adjunct professor at UCLA and National University:

Letter Grade	Percentage
A	96100
A-	90-95
B+	87-89
B	83-86
B-	80-82
C+	77-79
C	70-76
D	60-69
F	0-59

There are ways to make grading much faster, easier, and fairer — and as accurate as it can possibly be. You have already laid the foundation by outlining your grading policies and class assignments in your course syllabus. All of these pieces work together in helping you grade students. The more closely these pieces work together, the easier it will be for you to make fair assessments.

In your course syllabus, you outlined the student-learning outcomes. A learning outcome, you will recall, is what you expect students will be able to perform as a result of what they learned in your class. These learning outcomes, or standards, are not only helpful for you and your students; they allow your department to see how you will evaluate student performance. Your learning outcomes should be detailed and list concrete ways students will be able to demonstrate or perform the skills they have learned. This will help them understand your expectations. Your goal is not to pass judgment on students or compare them to each other. You want each student to grow and learn. To do that, set clear standards for what students will learn, and your criteria for grading them. The last thing you want is for a student to think they are doing "A" work only to find out they received a "C."

In fact, being able to evaluate yourself is also an important part of being a successful teacher. Enlist the help of your colleagues if you sense they are willing. This is your first year in a complex and challenging job, and to succeed, you might need to walk down the hallway a few times and ask your fellow teachers for their expert advice. Your peers can look at how your syllabus outlines student assessments, whether the assignments are relevant and challenging or not, and whether or not you are grading students' work based on the criteria you have established. A really brave first-year teacher might even ask a colleague to sit in on his or her class. While this might be a great way to improve your teaching abilities, remember that experienced teachers can also lend a critical eye to your student-learning criteria.

Specific Criteria

Having a list of learning outcomes is not enough. You must take the concept a little deeper by defining a set of standards, and also the criteria for meeting the standards. Start by looking at all of the components of your course, and then divide it down into topics. From there, write down a few standards or things you want your students to be able to do. Next, write a set of standards for what represents a good or poor performance for each of the standards. Finally, give these criteria and standards to your students so they know how they are being evaluated.

Students must also clearly understand your grading methods. If you are grading on a curve, tell them. The best rule of thumb is to stick to whatever grading methods you outlined in your course syllabus. If you change your grading policies midstream, you must guard against giving the impression that the change is unfair or shows favor to certain students. Last-minute surprises are a bad idea.

Unless your exams and assignments consist entirely of multiple-choice or true-and-false questions, grading is going to take some time. It would be nice to have an easy, fair, infallible, and perfect grading system, but it does not exist. Before we turn to the mechanics of how and what to grade, we will first look at some approaches to grading.

Foundations for Grading

Ideally, everything you grade will hinge upon everything you are teaching in class. It seems obvious, but it is easy to get off track with this. You want to give students the opportunity, through assignments, to excel when it comes time to test them on their knowledge. Students are not solely prepared to be good test-takers. While test-taking skills are beneficial, they are not as much of a concern as if the material they are being taught and the assignments they are being given relate directly to what they will be tested on.

Before you start grading, you will design tests and other assignments. The first goal is to design assessments that relate directly to what you are teaching in class. You have already made a good framework with your syllabus, and from there you can schedule the kinds of assignments and tests you are going to give. The assignments should be varied, just as your lectures and teaching techniques are varied. This allows students with different learning styles to showcase their talents, whether they relish the challenge of an exam, or shine by completing a long-range project. No matter what kind of assignment it is, your directions and expectations should be spelled out in detail so students have the best chance of successfully completing them.

Creativity can play a role in assignments, as well. These assignments usually take the place of mini-projects. They can include writing a variety of documents, such as letters, research proposals, case histories, or making a budget. Any of these assignments give students the opportunity to make a presentation and work on their public speaking skills.

You should also keep in mind how difficult the exams are. Giving nothing but multiple-choice questions does not encourage high-level thinking skills. For this, it is best to have them write short answers on exam questions. This will help students organize their thoughts and support what they say with facts.

Ways to Evaluate Students

Traditionally, education has relied on tests and memorization when evaluating students. Students try to memorize as much as possible in their quest to achieve the highest grade on a test. No doubt you have taken tests that have questions about minute pieces of information you would have no way of knowing unless you memorized them. The information is just not central to whether or not you understand the overall concepts and can do the work. If you want to be an accountant, being able to balance a ledger without errors is important. In contrast, knowing the date and time a manufacturer made an accounting software program is not a good measurement of whether a student would make a good accountant or not. Finding out who made a software program is not a skill; it is information that can easily be looked up.

Memorization cannot be entirely dismissed, however. If a student is not good at memorization, it might impede their success in college and on the job. Just remember that it is the teacher's job to teach students what the most important information is, and to teach it so students can remember the material. When memorization is the most important goal, testing becomes a game, rather than a measurement of how much is learned. Yes, tests are an inevitable part of college and must be mastered. It is a sad fact that students who blank out or stress out on tests are going to struggle much more than those who do not. Still, you can make the process much easier on your students by making all of your tests align as closely as possible with your subject. You must also consider whether you will use performance- or learning-based evaluations.

Evaluation styles

One style of evaluation is called performance-based evaluation. Aside from a heavy reliance on tests and quizzes, teachers who use these methods tend to have rigid rules, knock off points for late work, and offer extra-credit for students with lower grades. They might give points for class participation and develop a point system that allows students to bolster their grades with small tasks. A drawback to performance-based evaluations is that students might focus on ways to increase their points instead of increasing their knowledge in the class.

A more modern approach is the learning-based evaluation. This approach relies more on intellectual development and how students apply their knowledge, rather than on how many facts and figures their brains can memorize. There tends to be more flexibility and teacher-student interaction in this approach. In Chapter 7, we discussed evaluating your students' knowledge level. This sets the course by using what your students already know and adding the things you want them to know. With learning-based evaluations, you are more concerned with how students pursue learning. To do this, you must understand their strengths and weaknesses and what they hope to get from your course. When you start the class, give students a list of several of your main objectives. Once the class gets rolling, ask students if you are giving them information in a way that they can understand.

Rubrics

A rubric is a grading tool that provides a list of categories students must complete in order to receive a score. Allowing students to see the rubric gives them a better chance of producing excellent work. Students can even check their own work against the rubric before they hand it in. In the appendix of this book, you will find several examples of what a rubric should look like. Be advised that it can be a very time-consuming process to design a rubric, especially if you have never made one. Checking with a colleague is a particularly good option for this step.

You asked for a ten-page report from each of your students, and you now have enough paper on your desk to start a large bonfire. Now you have to read all of these papers — and grade them. Grading written essays and reports can be difficult because writing can be subjective. It is also likely that you will see a wide range of writing abilities from your students. Before you get down to grading the papers, you can do some prep work to make it a little easier on yourself. The quality of the papers will likely be higher, and the grading process will be smoother.

First of all, papers that are free of typographical errors and contain proper grammar and sentence structure are expected at the college level. Students should not get any additional points for this, but they can lose points for handing in sloppy work. Typos and sloppy work should never be accept-able, but there might be some exceptions in writing style. For example, if you are teaching a creative writing or poetry class, students might not be writing in full sentences.

The criteria you will use for grading papers should not be a secret. You want your students to know what is expected of them so they can succeed in your class. Here are some ways you can do that, as well as some tips for yourself when it comes time to grade assignments:

- Have a written criterion for what constitutes each letter grade for the assignment.

- Discuss the assignment in detail and explain what you want.

- Offer students an example of an "A" paper and explain why it deserved that grade.

- Have smaller writing assignments in class that relate to the larger assignment.

- If possible, meet with students to help them revise their paper. You might only have time to do this with the students who are struggling the most.

- As you are reading, pull out papers that you think represent every kind of grade. You can refer back to these as you go.

- Try reading through an entire paper before making comments. If you write while you are reading the first time, you might have trouble comprehending the material.

- If you get bizarre or nonsensical papers, set them off to the side. Save them for last. If you do not do this, you might get too distracted or spend too much time on them.

- Take the task of reading in small increments, or allow yourself a couple of days to complete it. You will pull your hair out if you try to plow through stacks of papers in one sitting.

The ABCs of grading papers

One approach to grading papers is taking a holistic overview, or taking a broader look at the overall qualities of the paper. You can do this by writing out the general qualities for each letter grade the paper might receive. For example:

- "A" papers illustrate a deep understanding of the assignment. They communicate and support a message succinctly, with clarity and confidence.

- "B" papers meet the assignment criteria and occasionally exceed it. They show an ability to think and logically present ideas. They have a good deal of the qualities of an "A" paper, but are slightly below that level.

- "C" papers offer basic information, but little analysis of the topic. They are generally well-written. There are some problems with the writing, including clarity or conciseness.

- "D" and "F" papers have serious issues in structure and content. A failing paper demonstrates the least amount of effort and understanding of an assignment, does not support its argument, and has major technical problems.

Grading with checklists

Evaluation sheets or checklists permit students to edit their papers using the checklist guidelines, and allow teachers to grade efficiently and consistently. However, some graders find segmenting the paper into specific items counter to their holistic understanding of writing. Others dislike using points that might add up to more or less than the grade the paper seems to merit.

If you are unsure if this technique will work in your class, ask your colleagues if they use checklists for grading. Also, ask if they can show you an example. Here is one example of how a checklist may be used for grading a project.

Consider whether a project met or exceeded the basic requirements you set. List the parts of the assignment that are most important. Then, use symbols such as ++ for superior, + for acceptable and a minus sign for unacceptable work. You will need to assign a letter grade for each of these categories. To be considered for a passing grade, all of the items you list on a checklist must be completed.

Grading with a checklist allows you to focus on the most important aspects of an assignment or a writing project. Checklists can also be given to students to help them get the best possible grade on an assignment. A checklist for a written science experiment might include the number of research sources required, what categories to include, and whether or not to use complete sentences when reporting the results.

Grading on a curve

Before deciding to grade on a curve, consider your department's policies. Essentially, grading on a curve takes into account not just the performance of an individual student, but that of their peers. Grading on a curve starts by looking at the highest grade received in your class, assuming no one made a perfect score. If the highest grade was a 90, you know that the top grade was 10 points below 100. You would start the process of grading on a curve by adding 10 points to each student's score. The final numerical scores can then be converted into a letter grade of A, B, C, D, or F.

There are pros and cons of doing this. On the plus side, if everyone does poorly, grading on a curve allows you to give the grades a little boost in the interest of fairness. If every student gets an A on a test, you can adjust the grades slightly downward. A drawback to grading on a curve is that it creates a disparity in student work. A high-achieving student might question why their grades are being used as a way to bring up the grades of the lowest-performing students in class. You might also ask yourself why you need to grade on a curve. Possibly, there are ways you can improve your teaching and raise scores, rather than having to grade on a curve.

Attendance

Be sure to check with your department for any specific attendance requirements. In addition to the policies you set, your department might have rules for the number of classes a student may miss and still pass. These rules can include distinctions between excused and unexcused absences — and how many of each a student can have. An excused absence might be a written doctor's note or a religious observance. Unexcused absences include oversleeping, feeling under the weather, or simply not being in the mood to go to class. If you have some leeway, consider allowing students a couple of unexcused absences. There are bound to be days they just do not feel well, or wake up and discover their car has a flat tire. Things happen.

Be leery of setting an attendance policy. Think back to your own college classes. You can probably recall some students who almost failed the class because they had poor attendance. Setting some standards is a good idea. Strongly urge students to make it to class and remind them that this is what they are paying for. What message are you sending them by saying they do not have to attend your lectures?

Assuming there are rules, or you are just curious about who is showing up, you will need to keep track of attendance. A few ways to take attendance include taking roll call and checking off student names on a sheet, assigning a seating chart, or passing around a sign-in sheet. Such tasks are easy to document.

Participation

Keeping track of student participation is more challenging. Participation can be more than answering questions or offering input during group discussions. Other activities are group projects, adding comments on your course Web site, or working through a complex mathematics problem.

Waiting until after class to write down who spoke or did something can lead to errors. A sense of awkwardness can result by taking notes while students are talking. If you must grade participation, design a matrix on a scale of zero to three, with zero being no participation and a three being excellent. Immediately after the discussion, jot down who spoke and rate their input. You decide on the minimum number of times a student must participate, while taking into account the opportunities they have to do so.

Formal Presentations

Many people despise or fear public speaking, but it is a skill required on some level in most careers. Remind your students that this painful exercise can help them once they get out into the real world. Nervous students can still succeed in making presentations if you outline specific requirements for presentations. Let students know exactly what you are looking for and give them steps for achieving it. You can grade students on how well they adhered to your set time frame, the organization of their speech, how well they factually supported the information they gave, their speaking voice, and whether they made eye contact or not. When assessing student speaking, tell them exactly how their presentation met or failed to meet the criteria you outlined.

Letters, Numbers, or Percentages

You must also consider what kind of format you are going to use for grading students. Policies on which format to use will probably be dictated by your college, at least when it comes to the final grades you issue to students. It is best to review your campus' own requirements. As a general rule, you might have to give a number designation to the letter grades you are using. Before you can issue a final grade, you must consider the weight assigned to all of your tests, papers, and other assignments (See the example in Chapter 3). Then, look at the grades a student received and assign a number to that letter grade. Take each number and multiply it by its percentage value. Do this for all of the grades. Finally, add up all of the numbers and convert it back to the numerical value for the letter grade.

You might give the number a little boost or drag it down a bit, based on other factors you consider for grading. If a student really improved and made an extra effort to participate in classroom discussion, you might boost the grade. If a student rarely showed up for class and was not very productive when he or she did, that might drag down the grade. As you learned in the section about disputing grades, be careful how you apply these techniques. If a grade is disputed, you want to be able to fully explain why a certain grade was given. You might also want to consider the impact it will have on your student. Dropping a grade from a "C" to a "D" can have a devastating effect. This does not mean you should go easy on students. Just make sure you can back up whatever you do. Often, you can refer back to your syllabus. You can use the following syllabus, courtesy of Dr. Eric Del Chrol (Chapter 18) at Marshall University, as an example of how to break up your grading scale:

ANCIENT SEXUALITY

(CL 471: 101, CRN 1815, Writing Intensive, Fall 2009)
MW 3-4.15, HH 403

Dr. E. Del Chrol   304/696-4323
chrol@marshall.edu   Harris Hall 412

Office Hours: Monday 1.30-3, Tuesday 11-12.30, Wednesday 1.30-3, Friday 9-10, and by appointment

---

Disclaimer

This course treats adult material in an adult fashion. Some of the topics will be controversial and difficult, and you may be offended by the texts, ideas, or discussion. The ancients are very different from modern America, and nearly every class will present ideas that will be different from, or will challenge, beliefs you were raised with or currently hold. We will at times be using frank and coarse language, describing sexual organs and how they are used, discussing acts of sexual violence, and attempting to understand sexual attraction, practice, and ecstasy radically different from contemporary norms. These topics will be pursued in a fashion appropriate to an academic and intellectual context. If you feel offended, you may come to the professor at any time to discuss your concerns and feelings.

Nonetheless, if you anticipate not being able to behave in an adult or academic fashion, or if you think your closeness to the topics of the course will make enduring it a trial, you may wish to find another class.

Required Texts:

Skinner. 2005. *Sexuality in Greek and Roman Culture.* (Blackwell)

Johnson and Ryan. 2005. *Sexuality in Greek and Roman Society and Literature: A Sourcebook.* (Routledge)

Green (Tr.). 1982. *Ovid: The Erotic Poems.* (Penguin)

Sullivan (Tr.). 1986. *Petronius: The Satyricon.* (Penguin)

Lindsay (Tr.). 1960. *Apuleius: The Golden Ass.* (Indiana University)

- Additional readings on WebCT. Note: Many assignments require heavy use of Internet-based resources. If you do not have a computer and/or fast Internet connection, please learn where the computer lab most convenient to you is.

Goals

Ancient Sexuality has two main sets of goals. The first set pertains to developing your abilities as a social historian, the second to articulating these abilities. As a Classics course, the Ancient Sexuality will focus on close reading of primary texts, though you will have the opportunity to use works of contemporary scholarship. As a Writing Intensive course you will have the opportunity to engage in frequent informal and formal writing assignments as a tool to aid deep reflection on complex and subtle questions. By frequently committing your thoughts to paper, you will improve your ability at argumentation and analysis. By doing peer edits, you will have the opportunity to see how others handle evidence and argue similar points as you (for better or worse). This course will have you enhance your writing skills and strategies, and aid you in your quest to produce thoughtful, incisive, well argued and well-edited prose.

Content Goals

At the end of the course, you will be able to:

- identify major ways that appropriate and inappropriate sex and sexual activity were constructed in the ancient world

- diagnose how those ways inflect and are inflected by historical, cultural, geographic, economic, and social factors

- articulate how those ways of viewing sex and sexuality intersect with and inform other social historical issues, like class, gender, status, and power

- explain how the ancient views of the above differ from today, and explain how contemporary values work in relation to the above

- problematize an author's assumptions to produce more inclusive readings of a culture

- lead discussion on topics you find interesting or important in a work of literature

- explain the meaning and significance of the literary critical terms above

Writing Goals

At the end of the course you will be able to:

- identify the characteristics of a thoughtful, incisive, well-edited paper that utilizes evidence from a work of literature

- edit another's paper, providing sensitive commentary and criticism on grammar, style, and content

- write thoughtful, incisive, well-edited, finished prose that utilizes evidence from a work of literature

You will:

- enhance your writing skills and strategies

- enhance your critical thinking skills through various forms of writing, informal and formal

- engage actively with the subject matter through various forms of writing, informal and formal

Grade

Your grade will consist of the following:

Project	20%	Term Paper	40%
Midterm	20%	Participation	20%

The PROJECT will allow you to interact with an important piece of modern scholarship pertinent to the day's topic. There are three components to the grade. First, you will summarize the article; then present your findings to the class; then demonstrate their relevance to the readings. You will be required to meet with the professor before presenting to ensure that you understand the paper and can formulate an adequate response.

The MIDTERM will be an essay exam that encourages you to synthesize the concepts from across the Greek readings.

The grade for the TERM PAPER will come in three stages, with three separate grades. Each stage of the process will be accompanied by detailed information in class on how to write, source, edit, and polish an exemplary paper. You will be permitted to choose a topic pertinent to one primary source from the Roman readings.

Points for your PARTICIPATION grade will be assessed from: evidence of thorough preparation (completion of and understanding of the readings); ability to complete In-Class Writing assignments; willingness to engage with the ideas of class orally. There are no right or wrong answers, just better and less well-informed ones. Be persistent and adventuresome: this is the key to success in this class and in life. POP QUIZZES will only appear when a student uses technology inappropriately. They will be difficult and you will be sad. See "Classroom Technology Policy" for more information.

ATTENDANCE is required. Unless you have "University Excused Absences," should you miss four classes, which is the equivalent of two weeks of class in a semester, you will fail the course. Even with excused absences, excessive absences are deleterious to your grade. It is far better to be in class than not.

THERE IS A GREAT DEAL OF READING AND EVEN MORE THINKING REQUESTED OF YOU. On average, YOU WILL BE REQUIRED TO READ AROUND 100 PAGES A WEEK. Please set aside an appropriate amount of time to prepare and reflect. Evidence of inappropriate preparation will necessitate you leaving the class for that day.

Policy for Students with Disabilities

Marshall University is committed to equal opportunity in education for all students, including those with physical, learning, and psychological disabilities. University policy states that it is the responsibility of students with disabilities to contact the Office of Disabled Student Services (DSS) in Prichard Hall 117, phone 304 696-2271, to provide documentation of their disability. Following this, the DSS Coordinator will send a letter to each of the student's instructors outlining the academic accommodation he/she will need to ensure equality in classroom experiences, outside assignment, testing, and grading. The instructor and student will meet to discuss how the accommodation(s) requested will be provided. For more information, please visit **http://www.marshall.edu/disabled,** or contact Disabled Student Services Office at Prichard Hall 11, phone 304-696-2271.

Classroom Technology Policy

Since the time of Prometheus, technology has been of ambiguous usefulness. Recently, the ability to connect to an individual anywhere has impoverished the immediate community of that individual. As such, this classroom shall be a technology-free zone. Any student who is caught using technology inappropriately, including, but not limited to, texting, receiving phone calls, or checking Web sites will cause the entire class to have a pop quiz. As mentioned above, these quizzes will be difficult and everyone will suffer for your rudeness.

What qualifies as inappropriate use of technology will be the sole discretion of the instructor. If there is a desperate need for you to receive a communication, please clear it with Dr. Chrol in advance. If you persist in using technology on multiple occasions, you will be asked to leave the class for the day.

- *ALL WORK WILL BE YOUR OWN, AND ORIGINAL TO THIS COURSE.* PLAGIARISM AND CHEATING IS UNACCEPTABLE. ALL SUSPECTED VIOLATIONS WILL BE DOCUMENTED AND PROSECUTED.

- *ABSOLUTELY NO INTERNET SOURCES MAY BE USED.* ALL THE INFORMATION YOU NEED TO EXCEL IN THIS CLASS WILL BE INCLUDED IN THE READINGS OR PROVIDED IN CLASS.

- *LATE WORK WILL ONLY BE PERMITTED IN ACCOR-DANCE WITH UNIVERSITY REGULATIONS.* NO OTHER LATE WORK WILL BE ACCEPTED.

Schedule

ASSIGNMENTS COINCIDE WITH THE TOPIC FOR THE DAY AND MUST BE COMPLETED THE DAY INDICATED.

Skinner = *Sexuality in Greek and Roman Culture.* The numbers after Johnson & Ryan refer to the selection number (not the page number). For example, Johnson & Ryan 1 refers to the selection that runs pp.19-23. WebCT refers to materials posted on the online component of this course.

24 August   **Introduction**

26 August

- Read Skinner Introduction (pp. 1-20)
- Parker "The Myth of the Heterosexual" (WebCT)

31 August   Epic

- Read Skinner Chapter 1
- Read Johnson and Ryan 1, 3, 5, 10, 17, 28, 43, 44

2 September

- Read Hymn to Aphrodite (WebCT)
- Project: Ogden "Homosexuality and Warfare in Classical Greece"

7 September   LABOR DAY: NO CLASS

9 September   Archaic Greece

- Read Skinner Chapter 2
- Read Johnson and Ryan 11, 13, 14, 19, 31, 45, 99, 134

14 September

- Read Johnson and Ryan 4, 12, 18, 24, 29, 47
- Project: Skinner "Why is Sappho a woman?"

16 September

- Read Skinner Chapter 3
- Read Johnson and Ryan 21, 22, 35-7, 39, 40, 97, 113
- Project: Hubbard "Pindar's *Tenth Olympian* and Athlete-Trainer Pederasty"

21 September   Classical Greece

- Read Skinner Chapter 4
- Read Johnson and Ryan 6, 7, 25, 32-4, 38, 41-2, 50, 51, 61, 62, 84-86

23 September

- Read Johnson and Ryan 88, 94, 106, 107, 109, 115, 129, 130, 139
- Begin Against Neaira (WebCT)

- Project: Kurke "The *Hetaira* and the *Pornē*"

28 September

- Finish Against Neaira, read Against Timarchus (WebCT)
- Project: Sutton "Pornography and Persuasion on Attic Pottery"

30 September   Hellenistic Greece

- Read Skinner Chapter 5
- Read Johnson and Ryan 48, 55, 72-3, 117, 135, 140, 143

5 October

- Read Plato's *Symposium* (WebCT)

7 October

- Read Skinner Chapter 6
- Read Hellenistic Selections (WebCT)
- Project: Parker: "Love's Body Anatomized: The Ancient Erotic Handbooks and the Rhetoric of Sexuality"

12 October   Review day/Paper topic discussion

14 October   MIDTERM EXAMINATION

19 October   Republican Rome

- Read Skinner Chapter 7
- Read Johnson and Ryan 8, 9, 15, 27, 30, 49, 64, 93, 112, 125, 136

21 October

- Read Ovid *Amores* (pp. 86-165)
- Project: Butrica: "Some Myths and Anomalies in the Study of Roman Sexuality"

26 October   Augustan Rome

- Read Skinner Chapter 8
- Read Johnson and Ryan 16, 66, 108, 142, 148-150, 160

28 October

- Read Johnson and Ryan 74-6, 82, 124, 144
- **PAPER PROPOSAL DUE**
- Project: Richlin "Roman Concepts of Obscenity"

2 November   Imperial Rome

- Read Skinner Chapter 9
- Read Johnson and Ryan 53, 54, 67, 79, 101, 116, 122, 128, 137

4 November

- Read Skinner Chapter 10
- Read Johnson and Ryan 58-60, 70, 81, 91, 102, 133, 138, 145-7

9 November

- Begin Ovid *Arts of Love* 166-266

11 November

- Finish Ovid *Arts of Love*
- Project: Davis "Arts of Love"

16 November

- Begin Petronius *Satyricon*

18 November

- Finish Petronius *Satyricon*
- Project: Habinek "Ovid and Empire"

23-27 November   THANKSGIVING BREAK, NO CLASS

30 November

- Begin Apuleius *Golden Ass*
- **DRAFT PAPER DUE**

2 December

- Finish Apuleius *Golden Ass*
- **PEER EDITS DUE**

7 December

- Read Skinner Afterword
- Read Richlin "Roman Sexualities" (WebCT)
- **FINAL PAPERS DUE**

19 October   Republican Rome

- Read Skinner Chapter 7
- Read Johnson and Ryan 8, 9, 15, 27, 30, 49, 64, 93, 112, 125, 136

NOTES FOR 19 OCTOBER:

Attendance

Mention bake sale

Debrief on test

- How could I have prepared you better?

- How could you have prepared better?

Skinner

Start by looking at a map

Conceptual problems with chunking

- (Greco+Roman)
    - o not just one unit of culture
    - o old doesn't mean the same!

- also not Greece then Rome, mixing of cultures
    - o Not just where one culture stops and another picks up
    - o Parallel Obama policies on terrorism with Bush – blending but different
- Etruria, Sabines, Phoenecians, Semites, East, West
    - o Mediterranean is radically diverse, lots of trade and cultures intermixing

Rome is inherently diverse, and that is a big diff from Gs

Description of Roman Social classes

- Diff with Man being all that matters, but the term Man as fraught
- PAGE 195
    - o Prob of patronage
    - o Slavery different from American South

Skinner's 3 big diffs from Gs

- Diff w/pederasty
    - o Free boys were entirely off limits
    - o Vs delicati
- Therefore no socialization, no real sig of relations with boys
- Visibility of women
    - o Adultery legislation
    - o Relig significance
- Sex violence and spectacle

Why was vice so scary to the Romans?

- Mil, relig, property problems

- Where did the bad stuff come from?

  o Money, the east, money means vice

  o Vice is foreign

Augustus' adultery legislation

- Wife gets tried

  o First legal status of women!

- Husb prosecuted as a pimp if he doesn't prosecute

J&R

Pull name out of hat to start discussion: How is the conception of love we see in the Roman readings different from what we've seen before?

DO COMPARISON OF CAT AND SAPH, 29-30 – HOW ROMAN DIFF G?

15 Odi et amo – crucifixion imagery in line 2, status and class stuff

27 Affection with wit, diff from G attraction

9 Tib: love helps adultery

125 & 136 Os impurum from oral

21 October

- Read Ovid *Amores* (pp. 86-165)
- Project: Butrica: "Some Myths and Anomalies in the Study of Roman Sexuality"

NOTES FOR 21 OCTOBER

Attendance

Remind bake sale tomorrow

Project on Myths and Anomalies

6 groups: Pick (claim) a poem from Ovid *Amores* and show how it is representative and rebellious against prior romantic ideas from class.

Late Work

When in doubt, refer back to your syllabus. By now, you can see that designing a good syllabus takes care of many issues that will come up in your class. This includes policies on students who hand in their work late. Cover whether students can turn in late work at all. Completely ruling out this possibility can make you seem too strict. Throughout your teaching career, there will be students who have legitimate reasons for extending a deadline. You should outline a procedure for penalizing late work in your syllabus and indicate what circumstances are viable for extensions. For example, you can stipulate that you will take ten points off for every two days that an assignment is late.

One of the arguments for never allowing late work is that it is not acceptable to be late for work, filing your taxes, or any other host of other responsibilities that come with being an adult. Therefore, this habit should be reinforced in the classroom. Yet some educators hold that the greater emphasis should be on learning. If a student hands in a mediocre paper on time, but hands in a stellar one two days later, is any harm really done? Only you can answer that question.

As a new teacher, handling a lot of late papers might cause a logistics problem. Consider that you will have to develop a system for keeping track of who handed in what and how late it was. It is not as though you need one more thing to keep track of. Also, having a written policy that allows late work will encourage students to take advantage of it.

There might be a way to compromise. You can set a timeline for how late a student's work can be. For example, nothing will be accepted if it is a week late. Or, you can write on your syllabus that being late will require at least one day's advance notice. That is almost like a little insurance policy that shows students have actually been doing the work, they just could not complete it on time. Ultimately, you want to keep your classroom running smoothly and allow a little leeway for the unexpected things that happen in life. As you gain experience, you might even start to find ways to speed up the time it takes to do things.

Speeding Up the Grading Process

For some teachers, this next tip will just be too stressful. Others might find it to be a strong motivator. Try using a timer or an old-fashioned alarm clock while you are grading papers. If you are allowing yourself 20 minutes for each paper, set the clock to that time. When the alarm goes off, you should be finished. If you find yourself taking too much time, an alarm can be a strong motivator. You really only have so much time, and an alarm will help remind you of this. Another way to save time is to stop wasting it. This means streamlining things that you have to do without taking the quality of work out of them.

Some ways you might be able to speed up the grading process include:

- Grade on how well your students followed the directions for the assignment.

- Consider whether every assignment needs a numerical or letter grade, or if credit can simply be given for correctly completing the work.

- Ask students to self-correct quizzes in class.

- Use a teacher assistant for straight-forward grading, such as multiple-choice tests.

- Plan time for grading so you do not feel so rushed.

- Use essay-grading software as a supplement to reading and grading papers.

E-mailing comments

An easy way to save time is to use your computer to make notes and comments for student work, instead of trying to write them out longhand. You can either e-mail the comments to students or print them out and hand them back with their work. Be sure to write the student's name within each file and use numbers to correspond to the comment you are making. You do this by writing a number one on the student's paper, and then writing "1," followed by your comment in the e-mail or on a sheet of paper. Another way to use technology to make comments is to make a tape recording and burn your comments onto a CD. This will probably work only with a very small group of students.

Explaining grades to students

Constructive criticism is a wonderful thing. However, you must be willing to ask yourself if your criticism is truly constructive. Is it helping students to learn and improve? Do not focus only on the negative aspects of an assignment. Grading should provide comments about a student's work that guides them into new ways of thinking and doing things. Offer some writing tips that will help them improve future papers. If you feel they are struggling with studying, give some pointers in that area. You want the students to improve and they want to get the highest grade possible. Remember to compliment your students for what they do well. Do not offer backhanded compliments. Backhanded compliments are when you bring up something they did well and then immediately comment on how the student failed. It does little to establish rapport and trust.

Balance is the key. Trying to do too much can backfire. Guide your students. Do not offer them a dissertation on every possible area of improvement. You will overload them with too much information, and they might miss the bigger picture. Try not to get discouraged. This information is offered only as a guideline. There is no way you will be able to do everything perfectly, whether as a new teacher or a 20-year veteran. Since you must critique your students, it helps to ask yourself how open you are to criticism.

Handling Grade Complaints

Imagine this scenario: You just handed back your first batch of papers. Then next day, you are whistling down the hallway on your way to class, feeling pretty good about yourself and how everything is going. Then, a student comes running at you while waving his paper over his head.

"How on earth did I get this grade?" he asks in an agitated voice.

"Wow," you think to yourself. "I didn't see that one coming."

Your blood pressure starts to rise and you feel yourself going into defense mode. You really do not need to be taken off guard by such awkward scenes. Grade disputes do not need to be played out in a hallway, in front of other students after class, or while walking through the student center. It is best to handle these situations in private. After all, your professionalism is being called into question, whether or not the student is correct. There is no need to panic if a student disputes a grade. Being a new teacher, though, you will want to keep the number of disputes as few as possible.

Your college might have a protocol that students must follow if they want to dispute grades. This can pertain to grades you give in class, final grades, or both. Always check to make sure what the procedure is for your department. Expect to get some complaints about grades. Large numbers of students will probably not quibble over a couple of points on an in-class quiz, but you never know. It helps to have your own policies for handling grade disputes. For example, you can have students write down why they are disputing the grade and e-mail it to you. It is much better than having a student chase you down the hallway while waving their paper over your head. You should also meet with the student individually to hear his or her complaint in-depth and respond to why they received their grade. Colleges prefer any disputes to be resolved by the teacher and student. When other people have to get involved, it means a drain on time and resources. If you decide to change a grade, you will probably be asked to fill out a form that explains the reason for the change. If you stand behind the grade, you might be asked to give the student a written response for why it was not changed.

If a student meets with you and is still not satisfied with your explanation, they might be able to take it a step further. Final grades for courses typically fall into this category. It can involve a very long and drawn-out procedure. In either case, there will likely be a written procedure that students must follow for disputing grades. You should be aware of what these procedures are, so you know what might be going on behind the scenes should a student choose to pursue action against you.

Often, the college will set deadlines for disputing a grade. If the student misses the deadline, they no longer have the right to dispute it. There might be a department head, dean, or a conflict management department that will handle any complaints. Sometimes, they will even guide a student through this process.

Check to see if your college has criteria that must be used when a student disputes a final grade. Often, they must have some sort of proof. Some examples might be:

- You made an error when calculating the grade and it resulted in a lower final grade for the student.

- There was no rationale for the grade. It was subjective or arbitrary.

- The student can show that their grade was lower than what another student received for the same kind of work that demonstrated the same level of competency.

Beyond this level, students can take their case up through the administrative ranks, possibly ending with a review committee. If the committee decides to change the grade after you refused to, that is not going to be the highlight of your first year of teaching. If an honest mistake was made on your part, it is best to correct it and move on. If a student is trying to bully you, it is probably best to stand your ground and allow the situation to play out. Allowing that to happen sets a precedent that can be difficult to break.

Allowing Yourself to Be Graded

You are not the only one who wields the power of issuing a grade. Your direct supervisor will assess your performance. Although you might not receive a letter grade, you can probably convert it into one, based on the comments you receive. Your students will also grade you, whether amongst themselves or through a formal survey. Sometimes you must turn the tables and allow yourself to be graded. Let your students tell you how effective they think your class is. You can create a worksheet or questionnaire that evaluates you on a scale of one to five in various areas. This can include your general teaching skill, the organization of materials, testing, and anything else you do in the classroom. The wording of the questions will color the kind of answers you receive. The numerical "grade" your students give you will be compared with other teachers. This might not seem fair, but it is likely to occur. Use the following template for your questionnaire to see if the learning outcomes you made in Chapter 7 were met:

Please answer each statement on a 1-5 scale:

1- strongly disagree, 2- disagree, 3- neutral, 4- agree, 5- strongly agree, N/A- does not apply

1. I came to this class with prior knowledge about this subject.

    1   2   3   4   5   N/A

2. The instructor adequately explained the process for solving these types of equations.

    1   2   3   4   5   N/A

3. The instructor is knowledgeable in the subject area.

    1   2   3   4   5   N/A

4. The instructor was easy to follow and understand.

    1   2   3   4   5   N/A

5. I can solve these types of equations on my own, with no help from an instructor or text book.

    1   2   3   4   5   N/A

Other

I am taking this class because: _____
_____
_____

Please identify two techniques to solve these types of equations:
_____
_____
_____

What was the most helpful part of this lesson?

_____
_____
_____
_____

Please include any additional comments below:

_____

_____

_____

Demographics (optional)

Gender

   Female   Male

Classification

   FR   SO   JR   SR   GR   OTHER

If you do not have time to make a questionnaire, you can simply ask your students to write the following on a piece of paper and hand it to you before they leave class: 1) The most important thing they learned, 2) the most helpful part of the class that allowed them to understand what was being taught, 3) any critique or criticism, or something that you did not do that was helpful. By doing this, you are measuring your effectiveness as a professor. You can see what worked, what did not work, and get ideas of things you can try for another lecture. If you choose to use a questionnaire, your results can be even more specific to the lesson you were teaching.

Honest answers are more likely if you do not ask students to put their names on the papers, especially if you are doing a survey at mid-term. Few students are going to offer criticism, especially if they know they will receive a final grade from you sometime in the near future. You can do this halfway through your course, at the end, or both. Your direct supervisor (most likely a department chair) will probably read the forms. They might also find their way into the hands of a hiring committee on your campus or at any institution you might apply at in the future. Chances are you will be pleasantly surprised by the comments you receive. However, if you receive a large number of "complaints" in the same area, it might be something you want to consider changing. Also, know the kind of ratings you receive will depend on the kind of students you have in your class. If you have many overachievers and you try too hard to be entertaining, it will be off-putting. Try not to worry about it beforehand, though. You have to adopt a teaching style and go with it. There is no way to be perfect in your first year. Even if you receive glowing reviews from your students, that does not mean you should not take a critical look at things you need to improve.

A drawback to using a rating scale in your teaching assessment is that it does not allow students to elaborate on what they are writing. Include a few questions with space that allows the students to write. You will get a lot more information that way. Some of the ways you can evaluate this are by asking students (or yourself):

- Is the material relevant and worthwhile?

- Are students learning?

- Am I doing my best to help them learn?

- Am I doing anything that hinders their learning?

- Have my students met the goals I outlined at the start of the semester?

- In what areas has their knowledge increased?

- What do they know now that they did not know before entering my class?

Finding the answers to these questions will take some soul searching; a critique of your learning objectives, exams, and assignments; and consideration of what you are asking your students to learn. In addition to asking for feedback from your students, consider asking colleagues for their perceptions. Particularly as a first-year teacher, you must be open to criticism and change. You will be a better teacher and your students will be better learners for it. Just as learning never stops in a place of perfection, neither should your teaching. You should always be looking for ways to adapt and expand your skills. After all, you expect no less from your students.

Being the best means being able to take a critical look at the things you are doing well and the areas that need improvement. A self-assessment tool is an excellent way to do this. At certain points during the year — and definitely at the end of your first year — take stock of how you are doing and where you can improve. You can even do a self-assessment before setting foot in your classroom. Take the time to consider your own unique strengths and how you can use them as a first-year teacher.

Chapter 13

Being the Best

You already have everything you need to be the best teacher you can be. Always remember to draw upon your own unique skills and talents. Knowing your own strengths is what will make you an outstanding teacher. There is no one-size-fits-all classroom format or personality style that is ideal for every teacher. Outgoing teachers who love working with students seem to excel naturally, as well as those with vast subject knowledge. All the knowledge in the world will not help you or your students without the proper communication skills to relay the information. Having said that, remember to be yourself. Do not worry about being hip or speaking your students' lingo, whatever that might be at the moment. If you put a genuine effort into reaching out to your students, they will respond. If you have a great personality, though, it will certainly help. You will be starting off with a great advantage over other new teachers.

A study by the University of Illinois found that some of the best teachers tend to have certain personality characteristics. The study found the best teachers are outgoing in and out of the classroom. They enjoy working with and supporting students. They are able to create a dynamic and exciting classroom, while also developing a strong rapport with their students.

Finally, excellent teachers can read their class while they are teaching. This requires a great deal of confidence, and the flexibility to shift gears or ad lib during a lecture. Coupled with that, they are not easily flustered and are able to keep focused on what they are teaching. Research shows there are several characteristics that can be used to measure teacher excellence. Studies point to teachers' knowledge of their subject, preparation for teaching, how much they expect from students, and their treatment of students. One of the top qualities of the best teachers is their knowledge and understanding.

Some of the most important qualities for teachers are:

Knowledge. The best teachers are experts in their fields. They actively participate in their discipline and keep up-to-date on the latest developments in their field. Rather than living in a glass bubble, they are avid readers and study what their colleagues are doing in their respective fields. Their efforts extend well beyond their campus confines. A quality that separates the best teachers from the average ones is how they apply their knowledge. They are able to synthesize history with current events. They question their own knowledge with insights that extend beyond the obvious. The best teachers also know that knowledge extends past having students who can do well on tests. They are more concerned with how students apply their knowledge, and how they use their knowledge to influence the way others think.

Preparation. Outstanding teachers are prepared when they walk into the classroom. They know time is too valuable to waste. When they prepare, the best teachers are first concerned with the learning objectives upon which they based their course. Every decision, whether it is designing an exam or a lecture, takes student-learning objectives into account.

Expectations. Top teachers have high expectations, but go beyond issuing as many papers and exams they can cram into a semester. Their assignments incorporate higher-level thinking skills and help prepare students for the real world.

Teaching techniques. The best teachers create a sanctuary for learning. It is a place where students examine issues in depth, solve problems, and examine their knowledge and opinions. This allows students to become active participants while learning, instead of relying on the teacher to "tell" them what they must learn. Outstanding teachers create an environment where students feel they are treated fairly and their opinions matter. Students learn how to be persistent and unafraid to make mistakes. The students are also given feedback that allows them to make improvements in their classroom performance.

Respect. Teachers who excel trust their students. They have a high opinion of why their students are in college, and they trust that students want to learn. Your experience might show that not every student sincerely cares about his or her education. They might be there to play sports, socialize, or fill up time until they decide what they really want to do with their lives. Until such time, you should assume every student is there to get an education. You do not want to color your opinion before you have a chance to work with them.

Self-evaluation. It is usually not fun, but it is necessary to assess your own performance and look for ways to improve. This is particularly true for first-year teachers, and it is a practice you should carry throughout your education career. As you already learned, asking your students and fellow teachers to evaluate you are just two ways you can get a critique of your performance.

Recognize that you are going to have struggles as a first year teacher. No matter how many setbacks the best teachers have, they continue to move ahead, confident in their own abilities. For a perfectionist or a high achiever, this can be the most difficult lesson to learn. Unfortunately, without a willingness to accept criticism from others or give it to yourself, your growth will be severely limited. Be willing to apply what you learn and move on. Do not be too hard on yourself. It is OK to have a bad week or make a few blunders in class. Recognize the mistake, learn from it, and keep going.

CASE STUDY: WHAT MAKES A GREAT TEACHER?

Lynne Farber, MA
Assistant professor, public relations
Florida International University's
School of Journalism and Mass
Communication

A great work ethic is what makes a great teacher, according to Florida International University assistant professor Lynne Farber. "I just always say I am going to go in there giving 500 percent. That is how I teach."

Though she makes significantly less money than she did in the corporate world, Farber finds her educational career "wonderful." Many of her students are paying for their own education and some are first-generation college students. She respects her students and treats them how she wishes to be treated, she said. At the end of one semester, her students gave her cards thanking her for making the classroom feel like home for them.

"They appreciate that I care about them, that I love them, and that I really want them to succeed," Farber said. "Each one of them is unique, and they all have different life experiences."

Farber recommends teachers be honest with their students. If a student has a question and an instructor doesn't know the answer, the teacher should say so. Teachers should show their students that instructors are human too. Students are more likely to respond when instructors use their real-life experiences in class.

As a beginning teacher, preparing to teach a class can be a very daunting task, Farber said. Usually, the first time is never perfect, but teachers get better at it.

"Asking what defines an outstanding teacher is like asking why a painting is beautiful. We can look at a work of art and know that we like it, although we might not be able to explain why," Farber said. "With this in mind, think back on your own teachers and why you liked them. Were they goofy, strict, serious, or enthusiastic? Ask some friends or family members what they remember the most about the best teacher they ever had. Chances are, all of these stories about favorite teachers will share one quality: They really cared about their students. What exactly does that mean? Is it being popular, running your classroom with tough love, changing mediocre students into 'A' students, or being a mentor? Being the best can mean being all of these things, and yet it means so much more."

Who Judges What is Best?

Now that you believe you have a good handle on what defines an outstanding teacher, you are pretty much free to put it into practice, right? Well, maybe not. You are not the only one who defines what it means to be an outstanding teacher. Your students and supervisors have their own criteria and expectations. This is important because you are there for the students, not yourself. You also work for the college, not yourself. It is a tricky balance to be popular with everyone evaluating your performance, while not compromising your own standards of what it means to be a good teacher. If the students like you and your class, word gets around. They are happy and your college is happy. Good or otherwise, what your students think about you is an important factor in how successful you will be. In Chapter 11, you read some of the things that students seek in a teacher.

To briefly recap, they want a teacher who:

- Enjoys working with them

- Has a great sense of humor

- Respects their opinions and allows them opportunities to express their viewpoints

- Can draw upon real-life experiences when presenting information

- Sets high expectations in the classroom and helps them achieve them

- Is down-to-earth and does not pretend to be perfect

- Is accessible and willing to talk with students about the class

Student opinion is important, but when it comes to job security, the most important thing will be the person in charge of your evaluation. If possible, find out the specifics for how you will be evaluated. Your college or the department you work in might have this information posted somewhere on its Web site. If such a policy exists, it will make it much easier for you to understand what your supervisor is seeking. You would think a list of duties or expectations would be helpful, but sometimes it is not. The form or policy on how teachers are evaluated will provide much more insight in this area. Some colleges might rate you on a scale of one to five by looking at several key areas. Or, a committee or an individual might provide a more detailed evaluation. Evaluations generally take place annually, although some colleges might opt to do a cumulative evaluation every three or five years. The frequency of the evaluations you receive can also depend on whether you are a candidate for tenure or not.

Course quality

This includes a review of your course design, including the syllabus, assignments, and exams. Some areas of consideration could include the relevance of the course materials. This can include everything from textbooks to handouts, and information from the Internet. Are your materials up-to-date and relevant to your course? Do they comply with college guidelines? The availability of materials, facilities, and equipment should also be taken into account when these areas are evaluated. You might get "extra points" for being particularly creative, or if you design a course that clearly shows how you will help your students acquire critical thinking skills. Being able to develop new courses and teaching practices are likely to earn you extra points.

CASE STUDY: A CREATIVE TWIST FOR THE CLASSROOM

Marlene Caroselli
Adjunct professor, UCLA and
National University

Creativity comes with age, at least for Dr. Marlene Caroselli, adjunct professor at UCLA and National University. In her few years of teaching writing, business, and education, Caroselli was named NYS English teacher of the year, perhaps because of the twist she has implemented in her classes.

"At my age, I have thousands of ideas," Caroselli said. And she has shared those ideas with other college professors and teachers of any grade level, in her 2006 book *500 Creative Classroom Concepts for Teachers ad Trainers*. For first year teachers, Caroselli recommends only trying a limited number of techniques — probably one a week or every two weeks. If the method works, then it can become part of the teacher's professional repertoire, she said. If not, then they can discard it and try a new technique the following week.

While Caroselli is filled with teaching ideas, she gives the following advice for implementing the concepts in her book:

1. Offer clarity and reassurance at the beginning. "I do this in a humorous way," she said. "I ask a lot of questions. But, if I call on you and you don't wish to answer, look me right in the eye and say "Pick on somebody else, lady!"

2. Switch activities every 15 minutes.

3. Allow opportunities for varied interaction: small groups, individuals, dyads, and triads.

4. Encourage participation from everyone and do not let any one person dominate or intimidate others.

> 5. Bring the world into the classroom: try a guest lecturer on a relevant topic, a newspaper article, or references to a popular television show.

Supervision skills

You might also be evaluated on how well you guide and mentor your students. For example, if you teach art, music, or dance, your students' shows or performances might be seen as a direct reflection of your teaching ability. A business teacher might be evaluated by how well their students perform while making speeches or presentations. As you gain experience, you might also teach graduate and postdoctoral students. In these cases, your ability to serve as a mentor and help to guide students writing dissertations might be examined. If your students win many awards, score highly on exams, or make other exceptional achievements, you will probably get kudos for that, too. Here, you thought just your performance was under review.

Student evaluations

Teaching to the test is discouraged in college, but be aware that your students' test scores might be compared to those in similar courses. Hopefully, some factors will be taken into consideration, among them class size, the number of students enrolled in the course, and whether it is an elective or a required course.

On the other end of the spectrum, what your students say about you could factor into your evaluation. If certain comments, whether positive or negative, seem to be surfacing a lot, this might be considered.

Portfolio

You might be asked to provide a portfolio of materials that will be used for evaluating your performance. Your teaching portfolio is personal documentation of your work and accomplishments in the classroom. For example, you may wish to include lesson plans that were particularly in-depth, or evaluations from your students about your teaching methods on a particular subject. Your portfolio should include a variety of things that will demonstrate your knowledge and skills to your current or future employer. You should also include your résumé and cover letter, along with copies of your certifications and any awards or recognitions you have received.

TEACHER'S TIP:

Continually add to your portfolio as you teach, keeping the most recent plans, evaluations, and other materials at the beginning of your portfolio so you have current samples of your work.

Since you have some control over this, make sure you have positive information that will help you. Also be sure to provide everything that is required and take note of any deadlines for providing the materials. During your first year of teaching, this might not be part of your evaluation.

Chapter 14

Problem Students

As a teacher, you have to make a stand. If students say or do something and you do not back up your policies, you will get pushed around. It is common to hear excuses for unfinished assignments from students who are bored, those who lost interest as the semester progressed, and those who really did not care in the first place. In addition to creating a dynamic, caring environment for your students, you must also create one where students feel safe — literally.

Your repertoire of safety measures should also include plans for how you will deal with severe cases. School shootings are not yet considered common, but they do happen. The overload of extreme stress and disappointment that college brings for some students, whether it involves grades or personal relationships, can have very volatile results. Sometimes, other students and teachers are caught in the crossfire. First, we will cover the kind of disruptions you are most likely to encounter in class, followed by some extreme cases of student violence. Although there is little that any teacher can do to deter random violence, there are many things you can do to keep your classroom running smoothly. Here are some of the garden-variety "problem students" you might encounter:

Class Clowns and Other Performers

Class clowns are one of the problems that can appear in a classroom. The antics of these students draw attention to them and make other students uncomfortable. Originality usually counts in the classroom, except if it involves causing a disturbance. Comedians are just one of the types of entertainers that can hinder your lectures. Some students cannot stop themselves from talking out of turn; they try to answer every question, or come up with questions of their own. One strategy to use is to put students into smaller groups so the number of people they are entertaining is greatly reduced. All the world is no longer a stage.

Oops, I Forgot

You reminded students for the past two weeks that their papers are due. The requirements for reading assignments are clearly communicated. Why then, do students arrive unprepared or without their assignments in hand? Call it human nature, or just the nature of some students. Holding students accountable for their work can reduce these occurrences. For example, you might ask a couple of questions about reading assignments. Refer to the syllabus and make other class reminders about when things are due. Students should be able to keep track of all of this, although a little nudge from you certainly cannot hurt.

Daydreamers and Ceiling Gazers

When students are not paying attention, they are often bored or disinterested. Perhaps they are not catching on. Maybe they cannot focus for long spans of time and take up doodling or texting instead of paying attention. Once again, revert to the syllabus. It is up to you to make expectations clear. It also helps to walk around while lecturing. Your voice will carry better and you will jolt some students into paying attention. Another technique you can use is to mention a student's name in the course of your lecture. Finally, allowing students to move around and talk to each other in discussion groups can help keep everyone awake.

Students Who are Ready to Give Up

The semester begins and students feel like they can achieve anything teachers throw at them. A few weeks pass and the work was more difficult than they imagined. Perfectionists can have the worst time. If you are teaching at a large college, a former valedictorian at a small high school might now be "average," a label they are not used to wearing. Some classes you teach might be exceptionally challenging. In these cases, it might help to have testimonies from prior students who successfully completed the class, even after they doubted themselves. If that does not work, perhaps a pep talk is in order. After meeting with a student in your office, you might discover that the problems have nothing to do with the class. Things outside of your class are impacting the student's performance. Chapter 10, you will recall, covered some of the ways you can build rapport. You should listen, without offering counsel for students facing a serious issues or obstacles in their life. Those things are best handled by counseling or other services available on campus that can offer the best intervention.

CASE STUDY: DEALING WITH 'PROBLEM' STUDENTS

Tom McGovern
Assistant professor of engineering
St. Louis Community College

What does an instructor do when he or she is confronted with a student who just does not seem to care about a class?

At the start of the semester, Tom McGovern, assistant professor at St. Louis Community College, will be a little more lax with due dates for assignments. At that point, students really do not know the rules, he explained. As the semester continues, though, he becomes more serious, and students who continue to hand in their assignments late face the full consequences.

"They must know this is not acceptable. This gives students a preview of how they will be expected to perform in the workplace. Assignments are due on the day they are due, not at some other time that is convenient for a student."

McGovern has also dealt with cheating students, excessive swearing by individuals, and inappropriate behavior in his classroom. The key to dealing with these situations is talking directly to the individuals at fault and helping them understand that their behavior is unacceptable. Sometimes, though, dealing with unsavory situations takes a little more ingenuity.

One year, McGovern taught a class in which a student was copying tests. "So I made two tests with exactly the reversed answers. When confronted with it, she denied it. She said she did all of her own work. One of the questions was whether the earth was flat," McGovern said. "I told her she could either withdraw or take tests separate from everybody else. She was seated in front of everyone else, so I could be sure it was her work."

Looking Inward

Recognize that your own behavior and attitudes might need an intervention from time to time. Sometimes you can fan the fire of your students' bad behavior without ever intending it. Allow yourself to consider these possibilities:

- Running your classroom as if it is under martial law can make students shut down. Being overly negative will probably not inspire students to "prove you wrong" or try harder. They might just stop trying completely. Remember, the classroom involves a partnership between you and your students.

- Picking on certain students, or calling on the same people again and again can lead to frustration for others who want to participate. If you are repeatedly disrespectful to a certain student, others will begin to wonder when it will be their turn.

- If you make a rule, enforce it. You damage your own credibility if you do not stick to the standards you set.

- Talking down to students can make them feel like you do not think they are capable of doing the work. Part of being a teacher involves being able to gauge how quickly students are catching on. Do not be too repetitive with basic information. Ask students to refer to handouts, textbooks, or other materials if they need to review what is said in class.

- If possible, do not discipline students in front of others. Take them aside privately and tell them they broke a rule. If you make a reprimand in class, you are more likely to receive an indignant reply from the student.

Extreme Violence

Extreme violence is far less common than verbal abuse and bad attitudes, which can be hurled at college teachers from students or their family members. At some point, though, you might encounter a student who is acting aggressive. A student might launch a verbal attack on you or other students in the middle of class. Experts say it is best to correct such behavior promptly, without responding in an aggressive way. First, allow the student to present his case openly, and then invite questions or comments. You might find out that other students are also upset about an exam, a topic being discussed, or whatever else might have caused the initial outburst. If two students are the focus of the disturbance, ask them to talk it out while sitting down. Now you have turned a negative situation into a form of a small group discussion. In the process, you are teaching the two angry students and others in your class the appropriate ways to handle and express their emotions.

A 2009 study by the Association of Teachers and Lecturers (ATL) found that nearly 40 percent of college teachers have faced an irate parent. The ATL surveyed more than 1,000 teachers, lecturers, and other employees at schools and colleges throughout the United Kingdom and discovered 87 percent of staff members had encountered a disruptive student. The good news is that almost 90 percent of these incidents involved minor disruptions — talking or daydreaming, for example. Disrespect from parents was a little stronger. About 40 percent reported being insulted by parents. Insults might sting, but they are certainly not deadly. Other situations can be much more volatile.

By now, everyone is aware of instances of violence perpetrated on college campuses. In April 2009, an 18-year-old college dropout shot a dorm monitor and a pizza deliveryman after returning to his dorm at Hampton University in Hampton, Va. All of them survived. Other college shootings have ended much more tragically. Also in April 2009, an apparent murder-suicide rocked Henry Ford Community College west of Detroit. Two students were found dead inside a classroom after police responded to an emergency call that shots were fired on the campus. One of the worst shooting sprees in history happened April 2007 at Virginia Tech. Seung Hui Cho shot and killed 32 people, and injured dozens more before killing himself. There is little that teachers can do to avert such tragedies, but being aware of the fact that these situations can happen, and knowing what to look for, can help raise a red flag for any signs of danger.

Of course, always act in the best interest of your students and your safety. It might be comforting to know, however, that the biggest "danger" in your class is not violence. Your students are more likely to cheat or plagiarize. Both of these acts can place their academic careers in danger.

Chapter 15

Plagiarism and Cheating

Degrees have been revoked, college educations have ended, and public relations nightmares have ensued. The fallout can be severe when student plagiarism and cheating are brought to light. This is nothing new, but that does not mean it is any less of a problem. In fact, it is a serious problem that can crop up in very creative, blatant, or subtle ways. It is likely you will have to grapple with plagiarism, cheating, or both, at some point in your teaching career. Being a first-year teacher could make you more vulnerable to such attempts if a student gets the notion that you will not catch on. You might get the idea that because cheating and plagiarism do not appear to be happening, they are not. Some studies say it is more common than most people realize. That is why it is important to look at how you can detect these problems, prevent them, and deal with them if they happen in your classroom.

Be warned that students can be very creative and sophisticated when it comes to cheating. Wireless earphones are one example. These virtually undetectable devices can be used to record key information on MP3 players, while the player is hidden in a pocket or a purse. It happened in China, where students used the earphones to cheat on national college entrance exams. A student at the University of Central Florida pretended to chew gum while she was actually talking to a helper via a wireless earpiece. Not many teachers would suspect students of cheating by using tiny pen or button cameras that can link into a computer. Think it cannot get any stranger? YouTube has a video that instructs students on how to use a computer to replace a nutritional information label with notes for a test. Then, the label can be printed and placed on the bottle as it sits on the student's desk during a test. Sometimes a device that is allowed during an exam, such as a calculator, can be used to cheat. Math students have learned to hide high-tech calculators inside the body of the basic calculators that are allowed during exams.

How can teachers prevent the use of all of these creative cheating methods? In addition to using plagiarism software, some teachers are using webcams to watch students while they are taking tests. An old tried and true method is passing out different versions of the same test during a class. The high-tech version of this is having students take tests on computers in secured testing centers. The best bet: Keep your eyes peeled for anything that looks suspicious, whether it is in class or a paper a student writes.

Colleges and universities that take strong stands against cheating and plagiarism do so because these things go against the very core of what they represent. When a student dons a cap and gown and walks off of a stage with a diploma in hand, it is a promise that they earned it by doing the work and meeting all of the requirements for their degree. Ideally, graduating from college also means they demonstrated an ability to take the things they learned and transform them into their own thoughts and ideas. As a teacher, you of course want to uphold these ideals. You will probably be required to uphold them. Know that if you try to protect a student and some sort of malfeasance on their part comes to light, it might be your own career on the line. You cannot stop a student from trying to plagiarize or cheat on a test if they are dead set on doing so. You can, however, protect yourself in the process and make it absolutely clear that certain things will not be tolerated. This can be done by outlining policies for cheating and plagiarism in your course syllabus, as well as on your Web site. Make sure you also review these in class and let students know the seriousness of either infraction.

Students who do either of these things can abruptly end their academic careers, not only at their current college, but also at any other college where they apply. Once an incident of plagiarism or cheating is recorded, it becomes a part of a student's academic record, following him or her everywhere. This record can still be unearthed during background checks with a potential employer years down the road. That is why you must be crystal clear to your students about defining plagiarism and cheating, as well as what the potential consequences can be. Mistakes are not considered acceptable excuses. Whether a student meant to plagiarize or not, the ramifications are usually the same. A similar "zero-tolerance" stance can be applied to cheating. A teacher might choose to punish both the student copying and the one allowing it to happen. The philosophy behind it is that the student being copied from should have been aware of what was happening.

Although the two can sometimes overlap, let us first look at some broad definitions of plagiarism and cheating. There are a variety of ways a student can cheat, including copying off other students' quizzes and exams, sending text messages with answers to themselves or other students, or getting answer keys from past exams.

Plagiarism is taking someone else's words, work, or thoughts and passing them off as your own with no attribution. There are different ways this can happen and, depending on the class and the subject, the approach to attribution can vary. In science disciplines, it is considered a cardinal sin to take the research or experiments of another and pass them off as one's own. If you are teaching a journalism class, for example, it is standard for every thought or quote to be directly attributed to a person, a report, a Web site, or other source used by either citing the source or placing it in direct quotes. On the other hand, facts do not have to be attributed. For example:

The attack on the World Trade Center towers happened September 11, 2001. Even if a student looks up that fact on Google, he or she does not have to cite it.

As you know, information is supposed to be considered credible and verifiable. Information gleaned from Wikipedia or a personal blog will not be acceptable, in most cases. There are many more facets to the standards of attribution for news reporting, but this covers the general framework.

The accepted standard for term papers or reports in college can be different. Depending on what is required by a teacher or the institution, direct attribution might not have to be inserted within the text of the report. Instead, it can be listed in footnotes at the bottom of a page, or in a bibliography at the end of the report. In the days of typewriters, plagiarism required a willful effort. Either an entire paper was retyped verbatim, or a set of papers from previous semesters could be kept in a file, with the name of the writer being changed each time it was used. The Internet has changed all of that. Virtually any block of text can be copied from the Internet and pasted into a document.

There will always be those who think they can beat the system, though. As a teacher, there are several ways you can combat plagiarism. Your college might even have software that runs a student project through a program that checks it against thousands of sources. Some of the programs can also be used to store student work and check it against the work of other students. After all, depending on number of students enrolled in different sections of the same class, it might be too difficult to check them all on your own. Detecting plagiarism is further complicated by professional services that write papers for students. The work might be "original," but it certainly did not come from the student who bought the paper. A student might slip you a bogus paper without you ever knowing it, even if you take reasonable steps to check it out. Plagiarism software only goes so far, and people who make a living by writing bogus papers are looking for ways around it. Some

Internet sites claim to provide papers that will breeze past any detection of plagiarism. Students can even hire a writer who will attempt to mimic their own writing style. This is where your own skills of detection become extremely important. Plagiarism might be more common than you think. At least one study shows that it appears to be quite prevalent.

A 2008 survey of 1,000 students at Cambridge University in England found that one-half of undergraduates admitted to plagiarism. The study, published in the student newspaper Varsity, found that some 62 percent of law students said they broke the plagiarism guidelines at the university. Interestingly, only five percent of the students who participated in the study said they were caught. Why did they do it? Students cited being overworked and looking for ways to cut corners. Now, here is something for all new teachers to take note of. Some of the students also said they did not realize they had violated the university's plagiarism policies. Is this an honest answer? The only certain thing it illustrates is why it is so important to make sure the policies are clearly documented in your syllabus, and are clearly explained in your class. In a written statement in response to the study, the university said it takes plagiarism as a serious matter. It also cited its policies and the stages of disciplinary action that can be taken.

A U.S. study by an expert on cheating showed business teachers should be especially leery of plagiarism and cheating. Their students are the most likely to cheat, according to Dr. Donald McCabe of Rutgers University. McCabe's 2006 report showed that about 56 percent of graduate business students have cheated at least once, compared to 47 percent of students in other fields. McCabe, who is Center of Academic Integrity at Duke University's founding president, used data from 54 colleges and universities to compile his research. The next highest percentages of cheaters were engineering students (54 percent) and law students (45 percent). Even these figures might be underreported, since McCabe drew only a 13 percent response rate from students. Students who participated in the survey said they plagiarized by making up figures, buying papers or having them professionally edited, using another students' work, or by not properly citing sources.

How to Find Plagiarism

You will probably recall some of the following examples of plagiarized work from your own college days. One of the most common indicators is a paper turned in that simply does not read like other work a student has submitted. Often, this is seen in the use of writing style or vocabulary. If some of the student's insights seem extraordinarily advanced — or they make no sense — this can be another tip-off. If you suddenly see some Shakespearean-like prose in a student paper, try typing a few words into a search engine and see if anything comes up. Finally, asking the student a few questions about his paper, you can begin to assess how much of the work was really their own. Students who lift things from the Internet can be a little sloppy with their work. Since a lot of material that is plagiarized comes from the Internet, here are some additional things to look out for:

- Papers that have a URL address at the bottom of the page. This implies the paper was simply printed off of a Web site.

- References to things that are not there. If a paper includes phrases such as, "Continued on page 12," or "See accompanying map," and those materials are not included, it can be a clear sign that the work is not original.

- If a paper only uses sources that are decades old, the student might have discovered an old paper somewhere that they are trying to pass off as their own. Unless the source contains information that is still considered highly relevant, old information can be a red flag.

- Referring to old events as though they happened last week. This can be a clue that the information was lifted from an article online.

- A lack of footnotes or a bibliography.

If any of these things arise in a student paper and appear suspicious, run it through your plagiarism-detection software. If something comes up, document everything before contacting your department chair, or even before confronting the student. Visit **www.plagiarismdetect.com** to try the free plagiarism software.

Students Who Plagiarize Themselves

Students sometimes might try to use old assignments from other classes in your course. If your students are writing about current events or an ongoing issue, you should ask them to change the wording they have used in previous papers and expand on it with new knowledge. In other words, they should not just take several paragraphs of text from previous work and slap it into a new paper. This does not show how their knowledge has increased. At its worst, self-plagiarizing can occur when a student takes a paper from one class and tries to submit it in another class. This is one example of how plagiarism and cheating can sometimes overlap.

Avoiding Plagiarism

As a teacher, it can be heartbreaking for you to watch a good student mess up their education because of a careless mistake. You cannot completely stop this from happening, but you can help your students avoid it. Tell your students that a lot of problems with writing papers can be avoided by effectively managing their time. By managing their time, the quality of a paper goes up, while their stress level and amount of errors go down. Students who wait until the last minute are more likely to make careless errors. Their work gets sloppy. Then, after putting an assignment off for a few days, they begin to wonder whether one file is their own work and another one is their notes. At the last minute, they might mix up the two and hand in a plagiarized document without intending to do so. Some of these problems can crop up if you are teaching freshmen or other students without a great deal of experience in writing lengthy papers.

Have your students honestly assess how long it will take them to write a paper. Experienced writers might be able to write a good 500-word paper in a couple of hours or less. But, if a student struggles with writing, waiting to finish a 2,000-word term paper over a weekend is a poor choice. Stress the importance of taking meticulous notes while doing research and writing. Students can document all of their sources on their computer, or by using index cards. If they are drawing information from a Web site, students should write down all of the URLs or copy them into another file. Whatever method your students decide to use, they should decide upon it well before writing their papers. This will save them time and mistakes in the long run.

CASE STUDY: HOW FIRST-YEAR TEACHERS CAN DETECT PLAGIARISM

James Ostrow
Vice president of academic affairs
Lasell College

One mistake when examining plagiarism is to view the act in an over-simplified way, according to James Ostrow, vice president of academic affairs at Lasell College. Rather than ask why plagiarism exists, teachers should examine what type of learning environment they are encouraging. This does not mean an instructor has done anything wrong; it simply means there is a disconnect within the student-teacher relationship.

"When you are engaged in writing about something you value, it does not cross your mind to plagiarize," Ostrow said. "First-year teachers in particular have to establish intrinsic values so that plagiarizing does not even cross their students' minds. Tell them this is their opportunity to express themselves. It is their chance to make a difference in the world. If they do not do that, then it is like saying their opinions do not matter. You have to strike them where it counts."

First, students must understand what plagiarism is — passing off another's ideas as one's own, Ostrow explained. Lasell College sends a letter to students every year detailing what plagiarism is and its potential consequences, which can range from failing a course or being suspended.

Lasell does not take a "cookie-cutter approach" to plagiarism, he said. Schools must strike a balance with the act, rather than only taking a harsh approach. "You have to talk about what actually occurred. We have a process where we meet with faculty and have them fill out a form. I think it is important to do that because then I have a file and I know if the student has done it again. A student can plagiarize one time and certainly can be suspended. It depends on the person." If a student is caught plagiarizing a second time, they are generally suspended, Ostrow said.

Cheating Techniques

Cheating on homework and tests is an act of academic dishonesty that has been going on for ages. It takes many different forms and some of them are more difficult to detect than others. One of the oldest ways of cheating involves copying off of other students during an exam or handing in someone else's work for class assignments. Some students will try use the work of a friend who previously took the same class. This is often detected by teachers, particularly if the first student did either an exceptionally good or exceptionally bad job on an assignment.

Another way students cheat is by paying someone else to do the work. There are a plethora of Web sites that sell essays and term papers on a wide range of topics. One way to thwart this is to warn students that all papers will be run through plagiarism checkers. This is fairly easy to detect, especially if the writing style is very different from what a student usually writes. If you strongly suspect a student has done this, run the paper through a plagiarism checker. The paper might have been sold multiple times. What if nothing shows up in a check, but you still suspect the work is not original? Even though it is not good to falsely accuse a student, it is even worse to never question a suspect paper. Talking with the student about the paper in question might be enough to decide if it is original work, or not. Proving it might be more difficult.

TEACHER'S TIP:

Students can use cell phones and MP3 players to cheat on tests, so it is best to not let them use these devices during testing.

Technology has given students many more creative ways to cheat. Bathroom breaks are often not allowed during testing for the simple reason that a student can look at a cheat sheet or use a cell phone to call another student and get answers. An MP3 player can be used to replay key answers or concepts during an exam. Students can also send answers back and forth to each other via text messages. A student resourceful enough to get a hold of your test might even be able to take a picture of it with her cell phone, and then work through the answers. Yet another creative cheating method is to scan a plastic soda bottle wrapper into a computer, print the wrapper and then write answers on the inside of it. This can be done with candy bar wrappers, as well.

For these reasons, it might be a good idea to ban water bottles, candy wrappers, MP3 players, cell phones, or any other devices during testing.

Similar to plagiarism, it is important that students understand the ramifications of cheating, which can range from getting a zero and failing a class to being expelled from the college. Make sure you follow all protocols required by your college if you catch a student cheating.

Reasons Why Plagiarism and Cheating Happen

The obvious reason for cheating is students want to finish their courses, get good grades, and graduate. They might cheat because they did not do the work, or believe they are incapable of doing it. Some teachers believe the best way to avoid cheating is to have many different assignments instead of one final exam or one major paper that counts for a majority of the final grade. A student who does poorly taking tests or writing might feel that cheating is their only hope of passing your class. With so much riding on one or two things, even a good student might panic and begin looking for ways to cheat.

One way to ward off plagiarism and cheating is to appeal to a students' conscience. Some teachers ask their students to sign anti-cheating or anti-plagiarism pledges. Probably the best thing you can do as a new teacher is clearly explain to your students what cheating and plagiarism are and why they are wrong. Tell them that doing research and crafting it into their own words helps develop their communication skills. These skills can then be used to help make a difference in the world, or used to write things that build upon current research.

Chapter 16

The Politics of Being
a College Teacher

Natural politicians are easy to spot in a crowd, though they are not always people who are running for office. Brilliant at the art of self-promotion, they create an air about themselves that seems to command instant authority and respect. People look up to them because they know how to get things done, and they always appear to have it together. Then there are those whose attempts at office politics always end in a bungling disaster. They tick people off without trying, can never seem to get support for their projects, and are always the last to be promoted, even if their skills are far superior to others. Maybe they were taught that "working hard and being a good person" is the way to get to the top. Sometimes, that can be a faster route to becoming a doormat. If you are on a tenure track, or even if you just plan to thrive and survive as a college teacher, you will have to learn how to play the game. This is not being phony. Think of it as learning the hidden rules of your institution's culture and playing them to your advantage.

TEACHER'S
TIP:

You must learn the hidden rules of your institution to be successful at politics on campus.

Every institution will have its own set of rules. The rules might even go against conventional wisdom. If you need to ask about something, ask. Many people will be flattered you came to them for advice. To a certain degree, though, only you can figure it out. Here is a situation where you can use your teaching skills to your advantage. One of the most important skills you have is being able to watch, listen, and observe. By doing these three things, you will go a long way toward avoiding political pitfalls. Here, we will look at a myriad of political problems, along with ways to avoid them.

Set Realistic Goals

If you just landed your dream teaching job, it is OK to view it through rose-colored glasses. Just be sure to clean the glasses a little and take a clearer view. As with any job, we tend to fantasize about how perfect it is going to be. Before we start, we have written the personality profiles of everyone we will work with and how supportive and cooperative they are all going to be. Then, reality starts to set in. You might not be given the exact classes you were promised or the schedule you thought you were going to have. There is a fine line between being assertive and being a team player. You do not want to appear to be a prima donna, but you do not want to be a doormat either. Every situation is different. If you were not given exactly what was promised in terms of classes, chances are that someone already knows that. Choose your battles wisely.

Be Nice To People in High and 'Low' Places

Powerful people can reside in the unlikeliest of places. Being nice to everyone makes you look like a team player and shows you are a pleasure to be around. In addition to that, consider how much easier this can make your life. Just a couple of examples are the department secretary and teaching or research assistants. Although you might consider it grunt work, you do not want your assistants taking that stance when they are gathering data or grading student papers. If you have treated the department secretary like gold, she is more likely to stay late on a Friday night when you send her an e-mail begging her to help you make last-minute travel arrangements for a guest speaker. Keeping good communication with the grant writers and alumni association is also important. These groups can become great allies, offering help with grants for your classroom or your department. Although people in the IT department or the janitorial team will probably not get you grant funding, their help can be priceless just the same. If your air conditioning breaks on the day when the temperature is 90 degrees and the humidity is 85 percent, you had better hope the repair crew knows your name. The same goes for the IT department when your computer equipment fails or you need to upgrade.

Be Sociable

Closely tied to being nice to people is the art of being sociable. If members of your department meet for a brown bag lunch every Wednesday, be sure to attend. When they ask if you can fill in for one of their classes, or they want you to read their latest article, happily agree to do it if you have the time. If not, your colleagues might not have the time either when you ask them to evaluate one of your classes. If you are perceived as being cooperative and the life of the brown bag lunches, you will have an easier time accomplishing your goals. Just as a reminder, be aware of the things that are most important on your campus. Reading someone's article might not carry the same level of importance as teaching, but it just might be up higher than you think.

Join the Club

The faculty lounge, or faculty club, can be a good place to hang out if you want to meet with colleagues and catch up on what is going on. If your college has one of these, it will probably be similar to faulty lounges you saw in high school. It is a place where people can eat lunch, grab a snack between classes, and enjoy conversations. As a new teacher, you definitely want to "see and be seen" on campus. You will have the opportunity to gain allies and learn a lot about the institution where you are working. If you teach math and there is a faculty group for math teachers, it might be wise to join. If your department chair asks you to lead a student math club, consider it. Again, the art of knowing what to take on comes from an understanding of what is important at your college.

CASE STUDY: THE POLITICS OF COLLEGE LIFE

Marc Cutright
Associate professor and director
of the Center for Higher Education,
Department of Counseling and Higher
Education
University of North Texas

In order for instructors to keep their careers alive, they must understand what is valued at their school. In some universities, research and public grants, rather than teaching, are the main areas in which tenured faculty are judged, according to Marc Cutright, associate professor and director of the Center for Higher Education, Department of Counseling and Higher Education at the University of North Texas. At community colleges, teaching is the priority and research might not be encouraged in the least.

When deciding whether to pursue tenure, teachers should consider the record of their institutions and what steps one must take in order to gain tenure. If it has been 15-20 years since someone has been given tenure, then efforts might be better spent in other areas.

New instructors should reach out to people, Cutright recommends. "New faculty members tend to latch on to a single mentor and follow them almost exclusively. Get multiple mentors. That way, you have guidance from a number of people. It can accelerate your career a little faster."

Being sociable also helps foster relationships with one's colleagues. Faculty want to work with individuals who are collegial and are going to make contributions to the school. "Recognize you are working with people who have good intentions and want to meet similar ends," Cutright said.

Yet, it is wise to be selective about the groups and committees when one is a first-year teacher. Faculty cannot take advantage of every opportunity. "Also pay attention to the kind of committee you are serving on and know what your role is. If you are serving on an administrative committee, you are basically there for advice. It is best to avoid controversial subjects as a new faculty member. Do not go looking for trouble."

In a similar vein, be sure to make contact with department chairs. Rather than viewing the person as a judge, make them an ally and ask for their feedback. But, keep in mind that no one is an ultimate authority, Cutright said, and if faculty keep asking for something they think will benefit the school, they will typically get it. The key is working as a member of a team.

"Politics is the art of getting things done. The people who succeed are usually not about power-grabbing. They share power. They take care of people, and the same thing is true of faculty positions," Cutright said. "If you can involve other people, and give them opportunities for success, they will include you in their success. For the most part, people want you to succeed if it is not at their expense."

Attend Big Campus Events

Any time a high-profile person is speaking on your campus, you should plan on attending, even if the topic is not related directly to your subject. It will probably be the talk of the campus the next morning and you will want to be able to get in on the conversation. Of course, that is not the only benefit to seeing a world-class lecturer. Chances are the information you hear will pique your interest in the topic. You just might even pick up some tips to use in your own lectures after observing how the speaker presented the information.

Toot Your Own Horn (a Little)

Call it an unfortunate fact of life, but the people who are good at self-promotion are the ones who tend to get ahead. No one is going to know about the wonderful things you are doing unless you tell them. Even as a new teacher, feel free to contact your college's public relations department. If you receive a grant they might mention it in the college newsletter or other publications. Some of these items also get sent in press releases to various media outlets in your community. News agencies have been cutting back on staff everywhere, and most frazzled reporters will not mind a couple of extra ideas for feature stories.

Choose Committees Wisely

Being an advisor to the basket-weaving club — unless you teach in the basket-weaving department — will be a waste of time for a first-year teacher. Remember to use your time wisely. You want to be involved, but you cannot spread yourself so thin that you burn out in your first year. Say you are a journalism teacher and are asked to meet once a month as part of an advisory committee for a new class that is being developed. Now, that will be a constructive use of your time.

Think Before Hitting Send

Never make derogatory comments about students or fellow faculty members in office e-mail, even as a joke. Tone of voice and intent are not apparent in e-mail. Your college's IT department will likely have access to your e-mail, and it might even be stored in a server so it can be accessed at a later date. Many people have been highly embarrassed, and a few have even been fired, over a misdirected e-mail. Depending on what you wrote, you might be in violation of college policies. You definitely do not need that as a first-year teacher. It is always best to not send questionable things. Accidentally hitting "reply to all" is just too easy to do. Now the person you were writing about has received a copy of the e-mail. If they do not think what you wrote is funny, you could find yourself in very hot water. These things really do happen.

Exercise a lot of constraint with how you handle your e-mails. If you feel the urge to fire off a pointed e-mail at someone, allow yourself to wait 24 hours before sending it. Often, you will be very thankful you never sent it. If the matter is urgent enough that you must respond immediately, send a very generic reply. For example, if a parent sends you an angry e-mail about a grade you gave his son, it might be best to send a reply stating you will be happy to discuss the issue with him over the telephone. Leaving a paper trail on hot-button topics is never a good idea. Again, the tone and intent of the words you write under those circumstances is completely left to interpretation. Do not risk it, even if a colleague started the exchange. An off-color e-mail coming from a tenured faculty member with 20 years at a campus will raise fewer questions than one written by a new teacher who has been on the job for one month.

Keep Your Promises

Information is power, and you want to keep the lines of communication open and flowing between yourself and your colleagues. Respond promptly to e-mails. If you take days to reply or never reply, people will think you are just not interested. You might also miss a very important e-mail this way. Some people communicate almost entirely by e-mail or text messaging.

The same principle applies to office hours. If you post office hours and you are never in your office, students might start to wonder why they even bother stopping by. Your fellow faculty members might wonder if you are out playing golf (even if you do not like golf). When you are established at your college, that is the time to leave an hour early on a Friday or allow a lunch meeting to last a couple of hours. New teachers in particular should show scrupulous work ethics.

Better to Stay Quiet

Here is a sad, but true, part of office politics. Before wading into gossip sessions, know the waters you are entering. It is easy to be swayed into criticizing or complaining, especially with a group of long-standing teachers who are talking about something that really raises your ire. You do not want to be paranoid, but sometimes people will try to get you talking just to see how much you will complain or what you will bad mouth. Then, the information is relayed directly to the person in charge of what you are bashing. Save the complaining for your spouse or a close friend outside of the campus. You never know who is going to overhear or repeat what you said. Gossip travels quickly, and it can be embellished or changed to suit the agenda of whoever is repeating it. You never know how information is going to be relayed. Until you are very certain of who you can trust, do not go there. In fact, you probably should not go there at all.

Mind Your Image

Students have been denied admission to colleges and have lost their right to participate in certain activities because of things they said or pictures they posted on social networking sites, such as MySpace or Facebook. The same applies to you as a teacher. A photo of you holding a giant margarita glass while wearing revealing clothing will not present a professional image. As with any job, remember that you want to be viewed as responsible. You do not have to give up having fun, just remember that camera phones and hand-held video recorders are everywhere. The next time you do something crazy, it just might end up on YouTube. Also, be aware that anything you do now might turn up years later.

Learning to Leave

What if you are working for a dean who makes you dread coming to work every day? When a supervisor has it in for you — whether you know the reason or not — it might be time to assemble a résumé and start looking for another job. Sometimes people who do not like you do not even know why they feel that way. If they are making your life a nightmare, be kind to yourself and start looking for another opportunity. The only other option is to meet with the person and ask them to tell you how you can improve. If your supervisor is not receptive to this, it is probably best to move on. You will be happier in the long-run.

Chapter 17

Research, Writing, and Publishing

If you were hired on a tenure-track, you will need to begin thinking about tenure while also learning to be a new teacher. As a first-year teacher, ask yourself if you are required to write, or if you are interested in being published in articles. Although tackling a major project in your first semester might not be wise, it is never too early to begin thinking about what you might like to write about.

> **TEACHER'S TIP:**
>
> Unless it is required, do not tackle major writing projects when you first start teaching. It is, however, a good time to start thinking about what you want to write.

Research, writing, and publishing are considered the foundations for achieving tenure. However, all college teachers should be interested in these activities, even if they are not required. All teachers conduct some form of research, even if it is only to keep up on current news and trends in their respective fields. Writing is another activity that is good for all teachers, as it gets your name out there and helps to establish you as an authority in your area of study. Books and articles are just two options, but if you truly do not have the time, you can also consider writing a blog. As always, check your institution's policies and make sure you follow them based on your career goals. Although much of this chapter will be geared to those seeking tenure, the information can be applied to any new teacher who is interested in research, writing, and publishing. This might seem like a lofty endeavor for a first-year teacher. A lot of it depends on your expertise in what you are writing about. If you wrote a master's thesis on the topic, or you have worked in a particular industry for a long time, you already have the base you need to write and research with authority.

You have already seen in the proceeding chapters that being a college teacher is no small task. Can you imagine having to conduct research, write scholarly reports, and publish them on top of it all? That is exactly what teachers on the tenure track are expected to do. You will essentially be doing two jobs at once. Now that you have been versed in the politics of teaching, make sure you understand the true goals of your institution. At a research-based institution, your work outside of the classroom might be just as important as your teaching. Of course, you will be expected to be a really good teacher. You will also be expected to be involved in the college. Still, if you are not completing the required amount of research or publishing the required number of books and articles, you will dash any hope of gaining tenure. Achieving that goal is often an all-or-nothing prospect. Either do everything that is asked and required, or lose all of the work you have done down the drain. Time management is an absolute must if you are going to flourish under these conditions. Use your time carefully, and start by finding out the true expectations of your college.

As already mentioned in Chapter 15 on college politics, you must find out the true goals and agendas of the institution where you are teaching. Ideally, you have investigated this before you ever start working there. That way, you will know the expectations and whether you are able to meet or go along with them. Said another way, if teaching is your one and only love, consider if you will be really happy at a college where research is the main focus. The converse is also true. If your dream teaching position involves writing books that challenge current thinking and you want to see your byline in prestigious journals, you might not be happy teaching at the community college level. Community colleges require little-to-no researching and writing. It is all about doing your own homework and carefully assessing where you want to work and where you are going to flourish.

Another point to remember is that it is never too early to think about publishing your work. This process can begin as early as graduate school. Graduate students are busy, but they will be even busier once they start teaching full-time. This is also a good time to co-author papers with established faculty members. Before going crazy writing as many papers as you can, ask if the papers you co-author will count toward tenure at the college where you plan to be teaching. If you are not on a tenure-track, you can afford to take more time with what you write. Whether on the tenure-track or not, being a published writer is good experience and it looks good on your résumé. You can best use this experience to your advantage later on by recording your role in researching and writing the papers you co-author. Now you are ready to begin preparing to write.

Publish or Perish?

"Publish or perish" is a common saying used when it comes to college teaching. Simply stated, it means that frequently publishing your work is the way to advance or maintain your college teaching career. The amount of pressure you will be under to research, write, and publish depends largely on the college where you are teaching. If tenure is your goal, or if you are working at a research-based college, doing these three things will be a requirement, or at the very least, an expectation. You may, however, want to write and publish your work even if it is not required. Doing so can only help advance your career, especially if you decide to move on to another college at some point. In addition, you will definitely want to conduct research, regardless of where you are teaching. Again, it will only help your career. At the very minimum, you should keep abreast of current trends and research topics in your field. That requires a certain amount of research. Are you ready to begin? Your first task will be deciding what to write about.

What to write about

You know you need to write, or you have decided that you want to. Now, you need some tips on what to write about and where to submit your work. Make sure you find out your college's qualifications in this area before you proceed. Journals tend to accept new, innovative topics. Writing textbooks is often not a good venture. The pay is not that great for the amount of time it will take you to research and write them. In today's world, you might even consider writing a blog. This can help with increasing your visibility in the academic world, assuming your blog is a good one. Later in this chapter, we will cover an entire section on blogging. For the most part, however, writing as a college teacher involves publishing articles or books. Some teachers do both, if they are prolific writers.

The first step is finding a topic that is timely, and one that you are passionate about. For starters, you might look at new developments in your field. The University of Maryland School of Law recommends teachers looking to publish their work consider law reforms. Another source of ideas for articles is to disagree with something written by a well-known author. For obvious reasons, some degree of caution is advised when doing this. A single presentation or workshop you attend will not warrant enough information for a book, but might help you create an article or a chapter in a book.

Finding time to write

Write something every day. This is particularly true when facing a large writing project. If you look at the total word count of an article or a book, it can be overwhelming. Set a limit of the amount of words you must write each day to make your deadlines. Some days, you will be able to do more than that. Other days, you might struggle to write 500 words. Remember to keep at it, even if it is just a little each day. Waiting until the weekend or waiting for a time when you have a few days off usually does not work. Inevitably, all of the time you think you are going to have will be taken up by something else. That is why it is so important to write a little every day. You must also make the best use of your time if you plan to finish your article or book. One way to do this is to organize all of your materials. Resist the temptation to jump into writing without getting yourself organized. When all of your research is complete and you are ready to write, use the outline as a guide to keep your thoughts on track. The outline does not have to be cast in stone, however, and you might reorganize the information or add and delete things as you go.

Marketing Your Writing

Be mindful of where you submit your papers. Make a list of potential places for publication, keeping in mind where your work is most likely to be accepted. Consider many different kinds of publications, whether they are journals or newspapers. Aim big and send your work to the best publications first. If they do not accept your work, continue moving down the list. If nothing else, this will allow you to get feedback from some of the top journals. Sometimes tenure committees will call a journal to ask what percentage of articles they accept. If it is a very high percentage, it might not reflect well on your quest for tenure. It is better to submit your articles to publications that are competitive.

You will most likely be marketing your own work, so pay close attention to the writer's guidelines given for each publication. Some might take e-mail inquiries; others might only take inquiries by traditional mail. Some publications might want you to submit the article, while others might want you to send a query letter first. This might depend on the size of your work. In the world of publishing, it is generally a no-no to send an entire book in with a query letter unless you were asked to do so. However, do not send off a great book proposal without having some chapters completed. If the publisher likes your proposal, they are going to ask to see some sample chapters. You do not want to be empty-handed, or you might lose their interest.

When marketing your articles, you should have an accompanying cover letter that explains why your work is important. Noting your intended audience is also a good idea. After you become skilled at marketing, you will be able to get maximum mileage out of the same article. For example, you could take an article you published in a journal, reduce it in size, and send it in as a commentary piece at another publication. Of course, as a teacher seeking tenure, you are doing much more than trying to get your name out there. With that in mind, it is always good to make sure that what you are writing will count toward tenure.

Publishing for Tenure

Any writing done for tenure should be prefaced with this question: Am I sure it will count toward tenure? If you have a mentor, you might consider asking that person for some advice. At some colleges, you might be required to have a mentor if you are on the tenure-track. In this case, it is likely a person will be assigned to you. Hopefully this person will not be on the committee that will decide whether you will get tenure. It is good to have a third-party person offering you advice. In part, this is because you want to have a free and open dialogue with your mentor. Make good use of the time spent with your mentor and ask him or her every question you can think of about how to go about getting tenure. You can gear your questions toward things that lead people to get tenure and things that cause it to be denied. This information can be valuable because it could give you insight into steps in the process that are not on paper.

Your college might have all of its tenure requirements outlined on its Web site or in the faculty handbook. As you enter the tenure process, research who the decision makers are and find the timeline for decision-making. Here are some additional guidelines for writing that can help both tenure- and non-tenure-track teachers:

- Keep jargon out of your documents, as the people reading it might not be experts in your field.

- Succinctly explain what you are doing and why the research is important.

- If you are pressed for time, or consider yourself to be a novice writer, co-authoring papers is another good way to start.

- Ask who has received tenure recently and find out what they have done to get it. Also ask if anyone who applied for tenure early has received it.

- Before accepting research opportunities or other offers, ask a trusted colleague if they think it is a good opportunity.

- Be smart about the papers and books you review. Try to limit them to a total of two or three a year and make sure they are in your field of study.

- You must keep records of everything you do while preparing for tenure. This includes everything listed above and all classes you teach, presentations you give, articles you write, and students you advise.

- Recognize that, as a new teacher, you are being closely watched. Do everything you possibly can to make a good impression early on. That is when an opinion will be formed as to whether you will be tenure material or not.

There is a big-time commitment that comes with earning tenure. Ask yourself how much you are willing to sacrifice and how it might impact your family life and free time. Make sure you are willing to make sacrifices and to manage your time efficiently. Without doing that, you are likely to burn out. For example, if you have small children or a new baby, your time is already going to be limited. You will want to figure out how much support and time you have from family members before adding any additional duties to your plate.

Right about now, you are probably not looking to add a lot of additional duties to what you will already have to do. Yet, you might want to consider writing a blog. Blogging is a good way to advance any career because it can be a form of networking. It might not help you win tenure directly, but you will be getting your name out there, possibly on a national level, which can help establish you as an expert in your field.

Blogging for Tenure?

TEACHER'S
TIP:

If you do not have time to write lengthy articles, consider writing an informative blog about your subject area.

A well-written blog can help give you visibility in your subject. Additionally, it helps keep you on top of the latest news in your field by writing about it. All of this might not win you tenure, but it can help to make your name known among colleagues throughout the country. You can promote your research and articles and explain to the world why they are important. If you are a well-known blogger, you might be quoted in national magazines, newspapers, or on local television or radio shows.

Blogging will let you develop a more conversational, casual writing style. Blogs are not written formally, and they are not meant to read like scientific journals. They are a place for you to show a little of your personality. They also keep you writing on a daily basis, requiring you to organize your thoughts or comments quickly, helping you become a faster, more efficient writer.

There are some possible drawbacks of writing a blog. If you write about controversial topics, you might offend people, including those who work on your campus. It might take you a lot of time to promote the blog and grow your readership base. You can spend a lot of time "playing" on the computer without getting your real work done. No one might notice the blog is there, and you might spend a lot of time trying to get to a higher rank on Internet search engines. Rather than spend a lot of time trying to make your blog more visible, you might want to enlist the help of some colleagues. This can be done when you write a group blog together. Writing a group blog is also a good way to get to know your colleagues.

Group blogging

If writing a blog on your own seems too time-consuming, you might want to consider a group blog. This is a good way to save yourself from feeling as though you must write a post every day. With several people writing, there will be a constant flow of postings, even if others are occasionally absent. A group blog is a good way to talk with colleagues about research ideas or other hot topics of the day. However, one of your fellow bloggers might write something particularly strange or offensive and you might get lumped into the same category as them. Another disadvantage of writing a group blog is that your writing might get lost in the crowd. To avoid this, make sure to develop your own writing voice from the start. Another thing to keep in mind from the start is the kind of working environment you really want to be in. For example, if researching is more your style than blogging, position yourself at a college that values research.

Researching

To get tenure, research will be required. Your teaching position might also require you to conduct research. Although this might not be a requirement in your first year of teaching, it is probably not too early to begin pursuing it. At the very least, you should begin finding out whether taking time to research is an option or not.

Even if you are going to work at a research institution, you should not automatically assume you will be able to do research. Significant negotiations might be required on your part. Your teaching schedule must be designed to allow you time to conduct research. There are two points to keep in mind in this area. Additionally, you might also need specialized equipment, additional computer software, or graduate assistants. All of these things cost either money or time. If you plan to do extensive research, you are most likely going to require a grant. Grants can come from your college, or they might come from an outside organization. Just as you did with publishing, make sure the research you are doing will count toward tenure. If you have been diligent and done everything you can to reach tenure, the time will come when the decision is made to either grant it or not.

If You Do Not Get Tenure

You published, but you did not get tenure. Now what? Your world will certainly not end if you do not get tenure. If you worked hard and it did not happen, of course it will be discouraging. Some teachers say that, depending on the college, you might not be able to work there anymore. Although it can be a huge disappointment, there might be some steps you can take to fix the situation.

One extreme "solution" is filing a lawsuit. Do not expect to win any job leads by doing this. In fact, you might find yourself banned from many teaching positions across the nation, although no one will ever tell you the real reason you are not getting in. Any institution is always leery of hiring a person who has filed a lawsuit against the place where they worked. People are afraid of getting sued because it can mean a lot of time, money, and embarrassment for the institution. There is also an unwritten political code that says you do not bite the hand that feeds you — even if you truly were burned. There will always be those who still feel compelled to stand up for themselves, however, and there is nothing wrong with that. Before considering a lawsuit, consider the potential impact on your career and the amount of time, money, and stress it is going to cost you. Even if you get a settlement, you will have to consider the cut your attorney will get. You should also consider the amount of time for work you lost by spending time on the lawsuit. In the long-run, you might make more money by simply looking for another job. Whether you win or lose a lawsuit, it is almost a nearly winless situation when it comes to seeking future employment. If you lose, it gives the impression the lawsuit was not warranted. If you win, you might seem like a threat to a potential employer. Your energy might be better spent in trying to find another opportunity and then making a graceful exit.

Once you file a lawsuit, a battle line is drawn. Your former colleagues, some of whom might have been willing to give you a shining recommendation, will probably keep their distance. In addition to leaving your career, you might also leave some friends behind. That can add to any sense of grief you might be feeling.

Any loss or disappointment can bring a period of grieving, which is entirely normal. If you gave it your all and still did not get tenure, you will probably feel a range of roller-coaster emotions. At some point, you will pick yourself up and begin to assess how to regroup. Debating the issue with family or friends is great, but only you can tackle your particular situation. Only you can ultimately decide the right course of action. While you are talking to people, you might also ask why you did not make it. Did you honestly think you had exceeded all of the requirements? Or, deep inside, do you know you did not give it your all? You might be in for some painful soul searching as you sort through all of this. If your evaluations were not stellar in the years leading up to tenure, the fact that you did not get it should not come as too much of a shock. If you truly believe you should have received tenure, you might consider looking into whether your college has an appeals process. A pertinent question to ask might be whether or not anyone has ever appealed and won after they were denied tenure.

Chapter 18

Wrapping Up the First Year

When the final days of your first year arrive, you will no doubt be a little tired and perhaps a little frazzled, but try to resist the temptation to coast through the rest of the semester. Assess what students will be doing toward the end of the semester and plan accordingly. If a final exam is coming up, allow ample time for students to review. Students might become stressed out, especially if the final exam counts for a large portion of their grade. You might also need to plan for a little more office time if you notice an increase in student requests to meet with you. Consider giving your students a handout (or you can post something on your Web site) about all of the key topics you covered in class. Some teachers even compile a study guide for their students. There is no reason to be vague or secretive about what the exam will cover. There is a lot of power in constructing an exam that holds the key to your students' academic futures.

Do not use obscure questions that will confuse your students. Keep in mind that the goal of the final exam is to reinforce what they have already learned. Tell your students what will be on the exam, and how large each section will be. If a portion of it is a short essay, let them know what you expect to see in the essay. You do not have to give away the topic, but tell them how the essay will be graded. Whatever method of review you choose, make sure it is effective for the subject you are teaching and the format of the test you will be giving.

Aside from the exam, you will also want your students to fill out their final course evaluation forms. Ask them to think back over the semester and assess everything they learned. You will have to determine whether you want students to put their names on the evaluations or not. Check with your department to see if a policy exists on this. Your college might want you to give anonymous evaluations. You might get more honest feedback this way — especially if the final exam has yet to be given. On the other hand, some students might not bother to fill it out and you will have no way of knowing. Explain why it is important for students to fill them out. Mention that you will consider what they say in designing future classes. You want to put the students in a helpful mode, not an overly critical one. You might want to leave the room and have a student notify you when the task is finished. Do not give back assignments and immediately hand out the evaluation forms. If a student feels badly about their grade, they might give you low marks on your evaluation.

You have no doubt learned that becoming an excellent teacher is an ongoing process, much like learning itself. You want to continue to grow, but do not be too hard on yourself. No doubt you will have many successes in your first year, but there will also be areas where you can improve. It is unrealistic to expect to have a perfect first year. Once the final exams, papers, and assignments have all been collected and the last class is officially over, you might want to put together a teaching portfolio to help record the successes of your first year.

CASE STUDY: THE FIRST YEAR IN REVIEW

Dr. Eric Del Chrol
Assistant professor
Marshall University

A lot has changed for Dr. Eric Del Chrol in the four years since he became an assistant professor. Chrol, who taught at George Washington University, the University of Southern California and the University of Maryland before moving to Marshall University, teaches a range of classical language and culture classes to both lower- and upper-division classes.

In his first year of teaching, Chrol planned everything down to the minute — literally. He was the epitome of being over prepared, and said he would stress about deviating from his lesson plans and schedules, especially if it meant a class did not accomplish all that he had hoped to. "I had time cues in the margins of my discussion notes," he said.

While he thinks that well-planned content is still important, he now spends more time on the method of how he will teach and get his students to understand the material, rather than on exactly what he is teaching. This way, he allows more space in his lesson plans for discovery — the moments when his students become engaged in the material and are actually understanding what is being taught. But, this lessened focus on content-planning does not mean that Chrol is under prepared. In fact, he makes a habit of including extra discussion questions and digression points.

How does he go about this? He has even worked a system out for that, too. He does all of his lesson plans, which are done in week-long blocks to increase flexibility during class, on the laptop that he brings with him to class. This way, he can easily ask and make note of what students have questions about, or rearrange lesson plans if some parts were not covered when he thought they would be. He also uses this as a way to take notes of his classes. "At the end of class I quickly jot down digressions and discussion covered so I can mold quizzes and tests to what I actually did in class, not just what I thought I would do," Chrol said.

In his years of teaching hot-topic courses, such as Ancient Sexuality, Chrol has developed a keen ability for developing bizarre student questions into teaching tools. Often, these questions or misconceptions represent misunderstandings of a concept that was not taught, or explained in the text, in the most constructive way possible. When this happens, Chrol psychoanalyzes himself or the teaching materials to figure out where the blockage is between the students and the concept. "The 'analysis' model is a technique that I developed over time, but early-on in my first year, I quickly learned the importance of separating the wheat from the chaff," he said. But, as he learned to distinguish the necessary from the lurid detail, he dramatically improved his efficiency and sense of control over the material and classroom, even though it took some time.

"I never believed my mentor when she said that the first year of teaching was harder than graduate school," Chrol said. "Finding my teaching persona, navigating the individual Byzantine regulations of the school, learning how to advise, developing tools that I would then use for the rest of my years — these were all quite difficult and took much more time than I had anticipated."

It was worth the time and effort, however, as Chrol remembers what he loves about his field and why he enjoys sharing the information with his students. "I think teaching can be the best feeling in the world," he said.

Teaching Portfolios

A teaching portfolio is a summary of the work you have done throughout the year. Some colleges will require you to compile a portfolio if you are a graduate student teacher or if you are on the tenure-track. At other institutions, the option will be left to your discretion. It is a good idea to have a teaching portfolio even if it is not required. A portfolio serves as a record of what you have done, and can give you insights into what is and is not working inside your classroom. You already have part of your portfolio prepared: Your syllabus, student assignments, and student evaluations. Your portfolio should also include a description of your teaching philosophy.

The teaching philosophy statement can give you a lot of insight into how you approach the classroom. Make sure the statement you make is completely original, to the point, and avoids clichés and meaningless jargon. Generally, it should include some of the experiences you have had during your first year of teaching. If you have difficulty beginning, consider starting with why you decided to become a teacher, or what lead you to your teaching position. What are some of the qualities you most respected in some of the teachers you had? What are some of the courses you would like to teach, and why do you think you would enjoy them? Writing down some of these topics will give you a good base of material that can be used for writing your teaching philosophy. You can include notes about classroom assignments, how you handled stressful situations, or positive notes from deans or students.

TEACHER'S TIP:

Remember to assess yourself at the year's end.

By the time your first year of teaching has passed, you will have a good idea of whether this is, in fact, your dream career. Hopefully it is. As you move forward, do not be too hard on yourself. You will have some time for introspection as summer arrives. Take some time to assess the good and the bad. Look over your self-assessments and assessments given by your students. You should ask yourself whether your students were learning or struggling. If they struggled, is there anything you can change, or anything you can do to increase student learning? If you can imagine yourself never tiring of asking yourself those questions, teaching might just be the ultimate career for you. Congratulate yourself upon completing your first year and realize that you have started a wonderful journey to becoming an excellent teacher.

Conclusion

By now, you know teaching college is a rewarding and challenging opportunity. Like any new career, you cannot expect to become an expert overnight. For some of you, teaching will come naturally, while others might need more time and training to truly make it work. Either way, stick with your goals and enlist the help of your colleagues.

As you learned from this book, one of the most important things you can do as a teacher is be well-prepared. This includes planning lessons, making sure your classroom technology is working, and knowing how to monitor and lead student discussions. Although every college is different, you also learned some tips to help you navigate the politics involved. Another important part of teaching college is learning how to identify trouble spots. Using the tips in this book, you can build a better understanding of how to interact with students and deal with difficult situations, such as students who cheat or plagiarize, and those who are not doing well in their coursework.

It is our hope that you move ahead with confidence and the utmost success. When that first student tells you how much your class meant to them, your hard work will be fully recognized.

Appendix A

Sample Syllabus

Undergraduate Department of Social Work
WEST CHESTER UNIVERSITY

I. COURSE: SWO 225 SECTIONS: 03 and 81
                            (Fall 2009)

II. COURSE TITLE: Race Relations [HBSE sequence]

                            (Fulfills "J or I": General Education
                            Course/WCU)

III. CREDIT HOURS: Three (3) Undergraduate Hours

V. PROFESSORS: Professor Chad D. Lassiter

                            Office Hours: T 1-3 (and by appointment)

                            E-mail: classiter@wcupa.edu

                            Office Telephone Number: 215-221-2794

VI. DEFINITION OF GENERALIST SOCIAL WORK PRACTICE:

This is a social work class, and therefore taught from a social work perspective. To familiarize social work majors and non-majors to this perspective, the program definition of generalist social work practice follows:

The BSW program at West Chester University defines generalist practice as practice that is grounded in a liberal arts foundation; upon which a generic and integrated social work knowledge base is built, and is informed by social work values. From this grounding, the generalist practitioner employs a core set of skills in order to effectively work with multilevel client systems in a variety of social work and host settings. These skills are rooted in the generalist intervention model, and include engagement, assessment, collaborative planning, implementation, and evaluation. Special attention is paid to the centrality and interactional nature of the helping relationship, and the ability to transfer the use of these skills between and among diverse contexts and locations. In this way, generalist practitioners are prepared to be able to engage, intervene, and evaluate outcomes with individuals, families, groups, organizations, communities, and larger social systems. Generalist practice involves viewing client systems from a strengths perspective in order to recognize, support, and build upon the innate capabilities of all human beings. Generalist practitioners utilize the ecological perspective, which draws attention to the effects and interconnections between individuals and their environments, in order to target the appropriate system for change. Generalist practitioners use methods that are informed by research. The goals of generalist practice include improving the well-being of individuals, families, and groups, humanizing the systems in which social workers and clients interface, and furthering the goals of social justice in society. [Definition informed by Landon, P.S. (1995). Generalist and advanced generalist practice. In *Encyclopedia of Social Work,* 19th Edition. Washington, DC: NASW Press.]

VII. COURSE DESCRIPTION, OBJECTIVES AND OUTCOMES:

This course meets the diverse community (J) or interdisciplinary (I) requirements for general education at West Chester University. This course addresses the Council on Social Work Education's (CSWE) education policy and accreditation standards (EPAS) regarding diverse groups in our society. The EPAS statements on integration and infusion of content about the experiences and contexts of people who are affected by institutionalized oppression (CSWE, 2001) are addressed throughout the course. This course presents a foundation and theoretical orientation to the importance of race, racism, and diversity in the day-to-day realities of people's lives.

This course takes an interdisciplinary approach and integrates findings from history, political science, sociology, and social work. It focuses on cultural differences as they affect family life, the development of law, and the nature and magnitude of racism in our society. The overarching goal of this course is to encourage the student to embark on the process of becoming culturally competent, where the student recognizes "an understanding of one's own world view and also those of the individual and communities with whom one is working" (Sisneros, Stakeman, Joyner & Schmitz, 2008).

The history of racism is examined not only in terms of the psychological and sociological pressures it exerts, but also in terms of its institutionalization through religion, education, health care, and politics. The course addresses issues of dominance and oppression. It explores ethnicity in a range of communities — from the African American to the Latino American, Asian-Pacific American, and Native American — including family structure, cultural traditions, as well as class, gender, and race ideologies. As it traces the interactivity of these different communities within the larger social fabric, it takes up issues of political/language discrimination as they affect such fundamental rights, equality, and due process for all citizens in the United States.

This course is interactive and utilizes group discussions and experiential activities designed to encourage "non-discriminatory" thinking and to stimulate effective communication by whites with people of color. Students are expected to participate actively and responsibly in group discussions, examining their own attitudes, beliefs, and communication styles in the process. The course objective is to develop understanding of and an appreciation for the struggles of people of color. The course objective of developing a foundation for cultural competency in the student, enhancing the student's ability to establish positive relationships with people of other races and ethnic groups is an intended course outcome. A more global course objective is to help the student recognize the importance of social justice concerns in the eradication of all discrimination in the United States (race, gender, religion, and class, as well as, discrimination on the basis of physical, age, mental handicaps, sexual orientation, or political beliefs). The course uses a combination of lecture, discussion, experiential exercises, and, at times, presentations by guest speakers who represent a wide range of distinguished voices on the issue of race relations.

For Social Work Majors Only:

LINKAGES TO OTHER COURSES: This course is situated in the Human Behavior in the Social Environment (HBSE) Curriculum sequence and lays the theoretical foundation for understanding the dynamics of social inequity, the history of racial discrimination, and the beginning self-assessment and understanding of cultural competency for social work practice. This course is part of the social work major's pre-candidacy coursework, and it provides opportunity for social work majors and those considering the social work major to assess their own readiness or suitability for the profession. All social work students are required to use APA style for writing. This course is required for all social work students. Social work students may take this course parallel to SWO 200, 220 and 300. The course is also open to other majors. Students outside the social work major are permitted to use APA or MLA styles for writing papers.

CONTENT ON DIVERSITY AND POPULATIONS AT RISK: The major focus of this course is on racial and cultural diversities, specifically relating to the four major groups and subgroups which have experienced institutional racism in the United States. These groups include the American Indian and Alaska Native, Latino-Americans, Asian-Americans, and African-Americans. Focus will also include some information on Women, Gays, Lesbians, Transsexual and Transgender, and Muslims.

CONTENT ON VALUES AND ETHICS: Professional values respecting diversity as a strength is the foundation to this course. Students are encouraged to examine their own values, views, biases, and attitudes toward people of color, as well as their own cultural and racial heritage, and to explore how these may positively or negatively impact their involvement with diverse populations. The ethics of cultural competency are actively explored through use of autobiographical journal, written assignments as well as through lively classroom interaction throughout the course.

CONTENT ON SOCIAL AND ECONOMIC JUSTICE: As students examine the bases of institutional and personal racism, they will also explore the broader issue of environmental racism and the role public social policy in impacting the quality of life of people of color. The history and development of Affirmative Action is studied in depth.

VIII. OFFICE OF SERVICES FOR STUDENTS WITH DISABILITIES:

If you have a disability that requires accommodations under the Americans with Disabilities Act (ADA), please present your letter of accommodations and meet with the instructor as soon as possible to support your success in an informed manner. If you would like to know more about West Chester University's services for students with disabilities, please contact the Office of Services for Students with Disabilities (located in Lawrence Center) at 610-436-3217 or 610-436-2564. If the student needs to set an appointment with the instructor at a more accessible location, a mutually accessible location will be arranged. Please do not hesitate to contact the instructor regarding any questions about assignments, due dates and course expectations.

CLASSROOM ATMOSPHERE:

- *Ally Statement:*

West Chester University's Mission Statement says, in part, "*We appreciate the diversity the members of our community bring to the campus and give fair and equitable treatment to all; acts of insensitivity or discrimination against individuals based on their race, gender, ethnicity, age, sexual orientation, abilities, or religious beliefs will not be tolerated.*"

Based on West Chester University's commitment to diversity, we believe that everyone in the classroom should feel safe. All social work faculty members attended the University's Lesbian, Gay, Bisexual, & Transgender Ally training and are committed to offering a safe space for *all* students, not just those who identify as LGBTQA. If you or someone you know would like to know more about this program, or need to speak confidentially about issues of sexual orientation or gender identity, please feel free to see me during my office hours.

- *Partners in Prevention Statement:*

In West Chester University's Plan for Excellence, one of the Student Success Transformation goals is to "improve retention, graduation and time-to-degree rates by assisting students during key transitional periods in their academic careers." All social work faculty members believe that many students do and will struggle with alcohol and/or drug issues that can compromise their success. I have attended a faculty/staff training program called "Partners in Prevention." This program was designed to help faculty/staff recognize the signs and symptoms of addiction and guide students to assistance.

IX. SOCIAL WORK PROGRAM OBJECTIVES:

This course meets the following Social Work Program Objectives:

Program Objective #1

Apply critical thinking skills within the context of professional social work practice.

Program Objective #2

Understand the value base of the profession and its ethical standards and principles, and practice values, standards & principles accordingly.

Program Objective #4

Understand the forms and mechanisms of oppression and discrimination and apply strategies of advocacy and social change that advance social and economic justice.

Program Objective #7

Use theoretical frameworks supported by empirical evidence to understand individual development and behaviors across the life span and the interactions among individuals and between individuals and families, groups, organizations, and communities.

Program Objective #10

Use communication skills differently across client populations, colleagues, and communities.

X. COURSE OBJECTIVES- Through this course:

COURSE OBJECTIVES	PROGRAM OBJECTIVES:	MEASURES:
1. The student will demonstrate knowledge of the historical perspective of racial and ethnic groups in the United States.	# 4	# 2, 4, 5, 6
2. The student will demonstrate knowledge of how oppression affects individual and group development across the life span.	# 4, 7	# 4, 6
3. The student will demonstrate a biological/psychological/social/cultural understanding of people of color.	# 1, 4, 7	# 4, 5, 6
4. The student will demonstrate knowledge of empirically-based research about the impact of diversity, including ethnicity, culture, sexual orientation, gender, class, religious beliefs, and disabilities as risk factor and/or resource, on human behavior and development.	# 7	# 1, 2, 3, 4, 5, 6

5. The student will demonstrate ability to integrate information about race relations from multiple perspectives to arrive at a holistic/complex view of how racism impacts human behavior in the ecological, dynamic, and ever-changing social environment.	# 1, 4	# 1, 2, 4, 5, 6
6. The student will recognize and identify the effects of federal legislation regarding people of color; ability to discuss the impact of many systems (e.g. health, housing, religion, welfare, education, justice, politics) upon ethnic groups.	# 4	# 3, 4, 5
7. The student will be able to identify the social and economic injustice related to unequal access to resources (i.e., health, education, justice system).	# 1, 2, 4	# 4, 5
8. The student will demonstrate integration of technology in completing course assignments.	# 10	# 4
9. The student will demonstrate increased self-awareness and a commitment to unlearning racism as a lifelong process.	# 1, 2	# 3, 4

XI. REQUIRED TEXTBOOKS:

Students should secure the following textbooks for this course, and social work majors must retain them for their reference library for future coursework assignments in the social work curriculum:

Healy, Joseph (2008). *Race, Ethnicity, Gender, and Class;* Sage Publications, CA

Tatum, Beverly (1997). *Why Are All the Black Kids Sitting Together in Cafeteria? And Other Conversations About Race;* New York, NY; Basic Books

(2000) *A Place at the Table: Struggles for Equality in America;* Teaching Tolerance; Montgomery, AL

(1995) *Us and Them A History of Intolerance in America;* Teaching Tolerance; Montgomery, AL

(1989) *Free At Last: A History of the Civil Rights Movement and Those Who Died in the Struggle;* Southern Poverty Law Center; Montgomery, AL

Recommended Readings:

Students are also encouraged to read newspapers, books, magazines, and attend various seminars, lectures, and cultural events in regard to racial and ethnic experiences during the semester in addition to all required readings.

United States Constitution; Government Printing Office; Washington, D.C. (can download from Internet)

Please note;

All work to be handed in must be typewritten; this includes work in the assignment book and journal entries.

Late work will NOT be accepted. Please pay attention to ALL due dates

XII. ASSIGNMENTS BINDER - Requires a three ring binder.
Please section and/or tab the binder using the following headers.

1. Assignment Binder (25%)

Due Date: Three times during the semester. (Each student will receive an exact week to hand in book). No later than 10/06/09 for first round; 11/17/09 for second round; and 12/01/09 for three and final round.

- *Section A* of **Binder -Journal Section.**

Each student is required to maintain a <u>typed</u> journal on issues related to race relations. Students are to journal and apply the new knowledge and terms learned in class, as well as document feelings and attitudes you discover related to race relations through discussions or material that is presented. By the end of the semester, students must have **at least twenty-eight entries in the journal**. Journals are submitted three times, when announced, throughout the semester.

The journal must include the following components: Your day-to-day thoughts, reflections, observations, and feelings related to course content. This may include reaction to readings, class discussions, videos from class, as well as events/happenings outside of the classroom, including news stories, campus events, interactions you have and/or observe between students, friends, and family members that are related to race relations. Apply knowledge learned in class and use race relations definitions correctly.

At least one entry per week minimum, resulting in at least 14 entries by the end of semester.

In addition, summarize at least one reading by highlighting what you learned from the reading and your reaction to the information. **End of semester a total of at least 14. Include information in the journal section. Remember 14 personal accounts and 14 readings equals 28 journals for the semester.**

- *Section B* of **Binder- Other Material Assignments and Definitions.**

All other assignments that are given in class are to go in the assignment book in section B.

Label all assignments, and please make a glossary section for (terms) definitions learned in class or through your readings each week.

- *Section C* of **Binder -Cultural Immersion experiences.**

<u>All must be completed by 12/01/09</u>

Students are expected to experience four events that offer them the opportunity to experience a **culture that we are studying**. For example, visit religious institution, an ethnic event or movie, spend time with a diverse family, or read a book (auto-biographical) over the course of the session. Write up your reflections and the issues and ideas generated from the experience. Include a section on what you learn from the event. Did the event challenge any stereotypes or preconceived notions or myths? Apply definitions and/or theories that you learned in class or through your readings to this experience.

Students can only attend immersion experiences from the groups that we are studying in class and only one event per group. Again students are encouraged to attend community events, plays, concerts, ethnic festivals, church, ethnic movies, formal lectures, restaurants, or read books approved by the professor.

(Total of four entries throughout the semester, relative ONLY to the groups that we are studying in class.) All cultural events are included in the binder under Section C.

- **Section D of Binder-Greatest Challenge Essay in taking this course**

Due 12/01/2009.

Write at least a three-page essay on the greatest challenge you have experienced in this course. Using the tape recording or writing you made the first week of class, reflect on where you "started," where you are now, and where you would like to "go" in the future in terms of the course content. Make two copies, one to be retained by the professor, and the other inserted in Section D to be retained by the student.

2. Family of Origin Interview Paper 10%
   ### Due 9/29/09.

Given that families are the primary "cultural carrier" in our society; conduct and interview the eldest member (i.e. grandparent, great aunt, or uncle) in your family system. Complete an essay (textual) based upon your interview and reading about your family's feelings on race and race relations in the United States.

Interview the oldest member in your family system. Ask them the following questions:

- Does the person recall the first time they became aware of race?

- How old were they, and what were the circumstances, and the message that they received about race?

- How would the older adult feel if you married someone of another race or ethnic group?

- How do they feel about race relations in the United States?

- What, if any, challenges do they feel the country must face to attain equality for all?

- What, if any, were the benefits for whites in the United States prior to the civil rights years?

- What, if any, were the challenges for people of color in the United States prior to the civil rights years?

- Did they feel that change (pertaining to race relation) was necessary?

- What information on race, or what message does the older adult feel is important for you to know and hand down in the family system?

In addition, explore and write up your own cultural heritage, through answering the following questions with the person you interview:

- Discuss what you have learned about race and racism from your family. What sort of impact does this learning continue to have on you today?

- Discuss how your family expresses its own cultural heritage (e.g., family traditions and celebrations, religious practices and customs, ethnic identification, etc.).

Through readings, compare how other families from your similar ethnic group feels about race relations (<u>YOU MUST Reference a journal article or book in this section of the paper</u>). Summarize your research findings, compare and contrast how different or similar your family is to others from the same racial/ethnic group in the United States.

Finally, concluded with your findings, summarize and state how you will attempt to explore your biases and develop your values in regards to race relations in the future.

YOU MUST reference all journal articles, books, and personal communications (the person you interviewed) on a separate reference page at the end of your paper. Papers that omit this vital information will be returned.

3. Profession Paper. 10%. Due Date- 11/10/09

A. Explore the issue of race relations within your chosen profession. Please interview someone from the profession (face-to-face or telephone interview) and answer all the bulleted questions below:

o   Have they noticed racism in the workplace?

o   Discuss cultural bias and how it is addressed/discussed in the workplace.

o   What are some of the abiding ethical dilemmas and current racial issues in your profession or career path?

o   How are racial issues being dealt with proactively?

o   Are there advocacy groups challenging the status quo in your profession?

o   What, if any, is your profession's formal stance on racism?

o   What, if any, is your profession's position on affirmative action?

o   How does the profession maintain cultural competence?

Critique at least <u>one empirical research study</u> from your discipline, i.e. social work.

Compare findings and discuss what you have found regarding race relations in the profession.

Conclude by stating reasons why, if, and how you will strive for developing a qualified yet, diverse workforce.

B. Writing and References

o   American Psychological Association (APA) format required for all written assignments. References are to be cited in the text and a list of references should be attached at the end of the paper.

o   YOU MUST cite your sources from relevant professional journals, conferences, and/or from verbal communications with professionals/professors/supervisors in the field.

o   Length: three to five pages, double-spaced.

o   Papers will be returned that omit this vital information.

4. Group Project, 20%. Random selection of your group will occur week III in class. Presentations dates are 11/17; 12/1; 12/8 and during final week if necessary.

A. Your task as a work group is to design a 30-minute, technological-savvy presentation for the class based upon the ethnic group the instructor assigns. Be creative and innovative; the objective is to introduce new strength-based information that few people know about your selective group. PowerPoint, taped interviews, You-Tube, and other technical support are strongly encouraged; please speak to your instructor regarding your creative ideas. The students may review key concepts in the presentation from the text and elaborate on key topics through independent scholarly research; students may consult with other students and/or student organizations of the groups that they are exploring for information.

o   A copy of the presentation and a list of references must be handed into the professor the week prior to the day of the presentation. Flash drive of presentation must also be downloaded the week before the group presents.

o   Every group member will be evaluated by each member in the group; every presentation will be evaluated by members of the class and the instructor using an assessment rubric.

o   All groups must compose a fact sheet and develop a short quiz (five questions) on important key points of your presentation that students should retain to distribute to the class. Make sure you have enough copies for each person in class. The group will grade the short quiz given to the students and report the grade to the professor.

o   Students may, but are not required, to bring a taste of food from the culture that they are presenting for the class. (Not calculated in the grade.)

B. All presentations must include contemporary facts regarding the ethnic group (reference all journals, books, and articles used to obtain knowledge); and relevant statistics census data. The group presentation must include a very <u>brief historical timeline</u> of the group in the United States, as well as state any constitutional rights the group was denied historically in the U.S. The major part of the presentation should detail obstacles and issues the group is presently facing in the U.S., strengths and contributions of the group in the US, interesting facts and accomplishments in various areas including but not limited to the arts, humanities, science, literature, and sports.

C. All references must be on the last power point, failure to do so will result in a lower grade.

5. Two quizzes, 10%

Online quiz dates during the week of **10/10 to 10/13;** and **11/19 to 11/21**, quiz must be completed by midnight.

6. Class participation (in class discussions) and attendance, 25%

Ongoing. Since this course relies upon student interaction, discussion, and processing of sensitive material, meeting once a week, class attendance is strictly enforced. Students are expected to participate actively in class, drawing upon readings, life experiences, and input from peers to test their understanding and comprehension of material covered. Class participation means coming to class on time and for the length of the class prepared to discuss and/or ask questions regarding the readings and actively engaging in the class. You **need to speak up** in class.

COMING TO CLASS IS JUST ONE PART OF CLASS PARTICIPATION.

7. Attendance is required for this course. If a student misses more than two classes, please see the instructor immediately.

The class meets once a week; one absence is like three, two is six, and three is nine. Any more than that means that you have missed more than one-third of the class material, which cannot be made up and will result in an "F" or a withdraw.

Attendance is critical; please sign all attendance sheets each week.

Attendance is not given for attending only a part of the class.

Arriving late, leaving early, and taking extended breaks results in missed class. "Excused absence" is a missed class.

PARTICIPATION	GRADE	POINTS
Active	A	100
Moderate	B	86
Minimal	C	76
None	F	0

• The final grade is dependent upon completion of all assignments.

   o **All work to be handed in must be typewritten.** This includes work in the assignment book and journal entries.

   o **Late work will *NOT* be accepted. Please pay attention to ALL due dates.**

XIV. ASSESSMENT:

The final grade will be based upon:	% Weight:	Learning Outcome(s):

1. Binder Book
  o Journal
  o Cultural Events
  o Greatest Challenge Paper
  o Other material & assignments
	(25)	4, 5, 10

2. Family of Origin Interview	(10)	1, 4, 5, 10
3. Professional Paper	(10)	4, 6, 8, 10

4.Group Project Presentation	(20)	1, 2, 3, 4, 5, 6, 7, 8, 9
5. Quizzes	(10)	1, 3, 4, 5, 6, 7
6. Class Participation	(25)	1, 2, 3, 4, 5, 10

PROFESSIONAL RESPONSIBILITY & CLASSROOM ETIQUETTE:

In classroom participation and presentations, interviews, and written work, you are expected to demonstrate:

- Respect for the dignity of others, even if you disagree with them

- Respect for confidentiality of information shared in class

- Acceptance of and respect for differences and diversity

- Intellectual curiosity

- Reasonable openness and honesty

- Respect for goal-directed group processes

- Accountability (meeting course expectations)

- A scientific attitude

XVI. COURSE OUTLINE

Weeks I-III: Understanding our Heritage
Taking a sociological perspective, these lectures focus on human origins and history; they incorporate material on historical time-lines and address the present political climate in this country. Theoretical material on working with the oppressed is intro-duced through the work of Akbar, Atkinson, Cross, Chestang, Dobson, Helms, Morten, Nichols, Sue, White, and others are used and serve as the framework for the entire course content. Students will apply the theoretical models to all material learned in class.

Week IV: The Native American

This section of the course addresses the politics of land acquisition, treaty violations, and forced relocation using as a focal point the Trail of Tears reservations and the sociological effects they had on native people. Group discussion will target understanding of Native American reluctance to mainstream.

Weeks V-VI: The African American

Beginning with the history of slavery and its effects on present-day African Americans, this section addresses discrimination legislation and judicial decisions, highlighting the Supreme Court decision Plessy v. Ferguson. African American family life and the way it differs from dominant groups is also studied.

Week VII: Latino/a American

This section focuses on the history of the Mexican and Puerto Rican communities in the United States, with an emphasis on language system and U.S. bias and stereotypes. This section of the course concludes with a discussion on Latino/a style of communication and the need to respect language differences.

Week VIII: Global Ethnic Community (Focus on Muslim Religion)

As more groups enter the United States, and as U.S. citizens live in other countries, it is critical that we understand what the inclusive meaning of a global community is by accepting others and adapting our U.S. communities.

Week IX: Asian/ Pacific American

This part of the course addresses the history of Chinese immigration law and takes the issues related to Executive Order 9066, which forced Japanese relocation during World War II. Discrimination law and its effects on Asian/Pacific family life are introduced, concluding with a discussion of Asians as the mythic model minority.

Week X: Work with your group on Final Presentation

Week XI: Women, Sexual Orientation
Information on the oppression of women in the United States and the issues related to sexual orientation that still occur in the United States is explored.

Week XII: Group Presentations and Relevant Discussion from the focus statement:
Focus Statement: As the course concludes, discussion each week on the social problems of today and their solutions will occur. Think if and what you would commit to personally, to increase the need for a more inclusive history that represents all racial groups; or how you would eradicate sociological effects of racism on class and ethnic groups, as well as on people with physical or mental handicaps or alternative lifestyles; and/or diffuse certain political barriers through equal rights legislation; or work to communicate across different groups to enhance social unity. Develop your action plan on race relations and be prepared to discuss your advocacy actions in class, during the next three weeks.

Week XIII: Group Presentations and Relevant Discussion

Week XIV: No Class, Holiday (Thanksgiving)

Week XV: Group Presentations and Summary Integration of Course (Reading of Greatest Challenge) Submission of Assignment Book and Greatest Challenge Paper due 12/1/09

Final Day: If needed, Group Presentations; Binders Returned, Grade Received via individual final appointments if no groups presentations are schedule for the final.

XV. WEEKLY COURSE SCHEDULE:

MATRIX OF COURSE OUTLINE, READINGS, LECTURES, ASSIGNMENT BOOK, AND JOURNAL ENTRIES

DATE	Class Lectures/ Discussions	Readings	Assignment Book/ Assignment Due Dates	Journal Entry
Week 1 9/1/09	Diversity in the United States Discussion and debate at the end of class.	For the next week read and takes notes from • Healy p. 1-138 cont. • Tatum, B. (1997). Part 3, p. 31-51 • A Place at the Table "The Strike for Three Loaves" p. 54-66 • Us and Them "In the City of Brotherly Love" p. 40-47	Audio tape or write about your feelings about Race Relations. Include your perceptions about race relations in the United States. Place the information in an envelope, seal, and sign the back and turn into the professor. DUE 9/08/09 Look up and place in your assignment book the following definitions with your reference, race, racism, racist, prejudice, stereotypes, discrimination, oppression, covert, racism, overt racism, affirmative action add new terms each week in section B of Assignment Book, study terms and use and apply terms in weekly classroom discussions, in your journal, papers, and other writings. Remember please add new terms each week in your assignment book. Each time your assignment book is collected the definition section is reviewed for the new terms. • Read Healy p. 1-138 cont. • Tatum, B. (1997). Part 3, p. 31-51 • A Place at the Table "The Strike for Three Loaves" p. 54-66 • Us and Them "In the City of Brotherly Love" p. 40-47 • ADD Census data on the racial make up of the United States and place in assignment • book section B Due 9/08/09	Journal entry and summary of readings

DATE	Class Lectures/ Discussions	Readings	Assignment Book/ Assignment Due Dates	Journal Entry
Week II 9/8/09	Assimilation and Pluralism Conclude lectures about theories relative to racial identity. Discussion and debate at the end of class	For the next week read and takes notes from • Healy p. 1-138 cont. • Tatum, B. (1997). Why are all the Black Kids sitting the cafeteria? Part 3 p. 31-51 • Tatum, B. (1997). Part 4, Ch. 8 "What do we mean when we say Indian? p. 143-153 • "Discovering My Whiteness" Posted on Blackboard	Place the following in your assignment book: Describe an institutionalized behavior you tried to break and place in your assignment book, section B Audio tape on your feelings of race relations due today.	Journal entry and weekly summary of reading
Week III 9/15/09	Wrap up of previous weeks. Exploring the legacy of Native Americans in the development of the United States Groups selected for final project. Discussion and debate at the end of class	For the next week read and takes notes from • Healy, Ch. 8 "Native Americans" p 261-301 • Us and Them "No Promise Land. p. 22-30 • A Place at the Table "This Land is Ours" p.44; "Against the Current" p.98. • Us and Them. "Blankets for the Dead p.14	Read "Discovering my whiteness" and " School Shootings and White Denial" write up your response in your assignment book in assignment book , section B Complete a Vision Quest and write this up for your assignment book, section B Due 9/22/09 Start Family of Origin paper due 9/29/09	Journal entry and weekly summary of readings Random Selection of Group for Final Presentation
Week IV 9/22/09	Exploring the legacy of Native Americans in the development of the United States Discussion and debate at the end of class	For the next week read and takes notes from • Healy Ch. 7 "African Americans" p. 139-260 • Tatum, B. (1997). Pp.31-75, Identity development Multiracial Families. p. 131-193. • Free at Last. p 1-104 (Free at Last-each student will receive a name of those who died in the struggle for civil rights and read and discuss in class)	Vision Quest Due Today	Journal entry and weekly summary of reading

DATE	Class Lectures/ Discussions	Readings	Assignment Book/ Assignment Due Dates	Journal Entry
Week V 9/29/08	From Slavery to today: Race Relations for African Americans and Inter-racial Discussion and debate at the end of class	For the next week read and takes notes from • Healy Ch. 7 "African Americans" p. 139-260 cont. • A Place at the Table "Who claims me"? p. 20-31; "Freedom's main Line" p. 32-43 • Us and Them. Harriet Jacobs Owns Herself" p. 30-39, "A Town Called Rosewood" pp. 84-92, "Riding with the Klan" p. 102-111. • Free at Last. Each student will receive a name to read and discuss from p. 1-104 Discussion of the name of those who died in the struggle for civil rights and read and discuss in class	Family Origin Paper Due Today hand in to Professor Conduct a survey on Affirmative Action Due 10/02/09. The design of the questionnaire will occur in class	Journal entry and weekly summary of reading
Week VI 10/06/09	From Slavery to today: Race Relations for African Americans and Interracial Discussion and debate at the end of class	For the next week read and takes notes from • Healy Chapter 9 Mexican Americans; Puerto Ricans and Cubans. p 303-346 • Tatum, B. (1997). Part 4, chap. 8 p. 131-143 • A Place at the Table. "A tale of two schools" pp.88-97 • Us and Them. "Untamed Borders" p. 76-83	Due Affirmative Action Questionnaire Due Today, place in assignment book section B QUIZ #1-On-line must be completed by 10/13/09 before class on 10/14/09.	ROUND ONE Journal DUE. Journal entry and summary of reading

DATE	Class Lectures/ Discussions	Readings	Assignment Book/ Assignment Due Dates	Journal Entry
Week VII 10/13/09	Latino Americans Presentation Groups Dates selected in class in preparation for final group projects Discussion and debate at the end of class	For the next week read and takes notes from • Healy Chapter 11, Arab Americans; Chapter 12, Future of Racial and Ethnic Relations in the United States, Chapter 13 12, Colonialism and Post Colonialism: The Global context of Racism • Tatum, B. (1997). Part 5, Breaking the Silence p.193-206	Discuss the implications of the Secretary of Education (United States) requiring all citizens to master two languages English and another language. Write up your response in your assignment book, section B, review your notes and information learned in class before you write up the response. QUIZ #1-On-line must be completed by 10/13/09 before class on 10/14/09.	Journal entry an weekly summary of reading
Week VIII 10/20/09	Global Community Discussion and debate at the end of class	For the next week read and takes notes from • Healy Chap. 10, Japanese Americans; Ch. 11, Chinese Americans, Filipinos, Koreans, Vietnamese and Asian-Indian Americans p. 347-384 • Tatum, B. (1997). Part 4, Ch. 8 153-156 • A Place at the Table "The House on Lemmon Street" p. 78-87 • Us and Them " A Rumbling in the • Mines". p. 48-57; Home was a Horse Stall" p. 92-101	Due: Profession paper- Due 11/11/2008. Develop an outline and plan, think about who you will interview from your professional, send an e-mail letting them know that you will contact them. Review the PATRIOT Act and write a position statement on whether or not you for or against? Place in the assignment section, include a response to the following questions. Does the constitution of the United States guarantee rights of all citizens born or naturalized in the United States? Should that be changed? Please review your notes on discrimination before you answer the question. Write your response in your assignment book, section B	Journal entry and summary of reading

DATE	Class Lectures/ Discussions	Readings	Assignment Book/ Assignment Due Dates	Journal Entry
Week IX, 10/27/09	Asian Americans and Pacific Islanders Discussion and debate at the end of class	For the next week read and takes notes from • A Place at the Table "Road Trip for Suffrage" p. 66-77; "Wheels of Justice" p. 108-117 "Going to bat for Girls" p. 118-127; "The Battle of Spanish Fork" p. 128-139	Discuss the Japanese Relocation Camps reviewing the constitutional denied rights that occurred and review your notes and include terms, definitions and other information learned in class. Write up in assignment book, section B. Start work on Profession Paper make an appointment to interview via telephone or in person with a professional from your discipline.	Journal entry and summary of weekly readings
Week X Work in Groups During Class 11/3/09	Groups work in class on final presentation	For the next week read and takes notes from • Us and Them" The Ballad of Leo Frank" 66-75; " A Rose for Charlie pp. 112-119; " Street Justice" p.120-127; re-read "Out of the Shadows" p.128	Work on Profession paper due 11/10/08 and Group Presentation Outline	Each group must develop an outline of each member's role and responsi- bilities and turn in to the Professor by next class. Your group may change the respon- sibilities by handing in an agreed upon change of plan sheet signed by each member of the group.

DATE	Class Lectures/ Discussions	Readings	Assignment Book/ Assignment Due Dates	Journal Entry
Week XI 11/10/09	Sexual Orientation and Women Discussion and debate at the end of class	For the next week re-read notes and class material and develop questions to ask during the group presentations	Professional Paper and outline for presentation due today. Discuss gay marriages and write a position on whether or not this is a religious, state or federal government issue. Does the Constitution of the United States allow all gay men and lesbian to marry? Is marriage a state or federal law? Should it be changed? Please review your notes on oppression before you answer the question. Write up your response in your assignment book, section B.	Round TWO Journals DUE Journal entry and summary of weekly readings
Week XII 11/17/09	GROUP PRESENTA-TIONS and Discussions (2) Quiz Posted Discussion on focus statements.	Complete classroom work and discuss your action plan to increase awareness of race rela-tions in the future.	Ask questions based on readings and informa-tion learned in class. Quiz #2 Online by 11/18 to 11/21/09	Journal entry and summary of weekly readings
Week XIII 11/27/09 NO Class	No Class Happy Holiday	Complete classroom work	Complete Assignment Book and Cultural Events (3)	Journal entry and summary of weekly readings
Week XIV 12/01/09	GROUP PRESENTA-TIONS and Discussions (2) Discussion on focus statements.	Complete classroom work and discuss your action plan to increase awareness of race rela-tions in the future.	Ask questions based on readings and informa-tion learned in class Greatest Challenge Paper Due Turn in Binder for Final Grading	Round THREE FINAL Journal DUE Journal entry and summary of weekly readings

DATE	Class Lectures/ Discussions	Readings	Assignment Book/ Assignment Due Dates	Journal Entry
Week XV 12/08/09	GROUP PRESENTA-TIONS and Discussions (2) Discussion on focus statements. Read a section of your greatest challenge in the final class and answers the question how we all can have a place at the table in the United States?	Complete classroom work and discuss your action plan to increase awareness of race relations in the future.	Ask questions based on readings and information learned in class	Last Class Get appointment time for final grade during final week.
Final Time (if necessary, final presentations, if not, students will make an appointment with professor to pick up their assignment book.	GROUP PRESENTA-TIONS and Discussions Discussion on the groups at the end of class =If we have class. Read a section of your greatest challenge in the final class and answers the question how we all can have a place at the table in the United States?	Apply Reading and Information Learned in Class	Ask questions based on readings and information learned in class	Assignment books returned.

Please note: If classes are cancelled due to inclement weather, all assignments are due on the date(s) in the outline. However, you may hand the assignments in at the next class session.

XVI. EXPECTATIONS OF PROFESSIONAL BEHAVIOR

All Social Work Majors or intended Majors are expected to demonstrate the following basic abilities:

- **Professional Behavior**

  Exhibits behaviors that are in compliance with program policies, institutional policies, professional ethical standards, and societal laws in classroom, field, and community. Appearance, dress, and general demeanor reflect a professional manner. Shows potential for responsible and accountable behavior by knowing and practicing within the scope of social work, respecting others, being punctual and dependable, prioritizing responsibilities, attending class regularly, observing deadlines, completing assignments on time, keeping appointments or making appropriate arrangements, and accepting supervision and criticism in a positive manner. Works effectively with others, regardless of level of authority. Advocates for him/her in an appropriate and responsible manner and uses proper channels for conflict resolution. Shows a willingness to receive and accept feedback and supervision in a positive manner, as well as use such feedback to enhance professional development.

- **Self-Awareness**

  Exhibits knowledge of how one's values, attitudes, beliefs, emotions, and past experiences affect thinking, behavior, and relationships. Accurately assesses one's own strengths, limitations, and suitability for professional practice. Shows awareness of self and how one is perceived by others. Reflects on one's own limitations as they relate to professional capacities. Is willing to examine and change behavior when it interferes in working with clients and other professionals.

- **Communication Skills**

  Demonstrates sufficient written and oral skills to comprehend information and communicate ideas and feelings.

a) _Written_: Writes clearly, uses correct grammar and spelling, and applies appropriate writing style, including American Psychological Association (APA) referencing, appropriate source citation, and documentation. Demonstrates sufficient skills in written English to understand content presented in the program and to complete adequately all written assignments, as specified by faculty.

b) _Oral_: Communicates effectively and sensitively with other students, faculty, staff, clients, and professionals. Expresses ideas and feelings clearly, and demonstrates a willingness and ability to listen to others. Demonstrates sufficient skills in spoken English to understand content presented in the program, to complete adequately all oral assignments, and to meet the objectives of field placement experiences, as specified by faculty.

- **Interpersonal Skills:**

  Demonstrates the interpersonal skills needed to relate effectively to other students, faculty, staff, clients, and professionals and to fulfill the ethical obligations of the profession. These include compassion, empathy, altruism, integrity, and demonstration of respect for and consideration of others. Takes appropriate responsibility for own actions and considers the impact of these actions on others.

- **Cognitive Skills**

  Exhibits sufficient knowledge of social work and clarity of thinking to process information and apply it to appropriate situations in classroom and field. Demonstrates grounding in relevant social, behavioral, and biological science knowledge and research, including knowledge and skills in relationship building, data gathering, assessment, intervention, and evaluation of practice. Exhibits ability to conceptualize and integrate knowledge and apply that knowledge to professional practice.

- **Stress Management**

  Demonstrates ability to deal with current life stressors through the use of appropriate coping mechanisms. Handles stress effectively by using appropriate self-care and developing supportive relationships with colleagues, peers, and others.

- **Emotional and Mental Capacities**

  Uses sound judgment. Seeks and effectively uses help for medical or emotional problems that interfere with scholastic and professional performance. Engages in counseling or seeks out support and help if personal problems, psychosocial distress, substance abuse, or mental health difficulties do any of the following:

  o   compromise scholastic or other performance

  o   interfere with professional judgment and behavior

  o   jeopardize the best interests of those to whom the social work student has a professional responsibility (as outlined in the current Codes of Ethics by the National Association of Social Workers and the PA State Board of Social Worker Examiners for Social Work Licensure).

- **Professional Commitment**

  Exhibits a strong commitment to the goals of social work and to the ethical standards of the profession, as specified in the NASW Code of Ethics and the Code of Ethics for Social Work Licensure in Pennsylvania. Demonstrates commitment to the essential values of social work that includes the respect for the dignity and worth of every individual and his/her right to a just share of society's resources (social justice).

- **Ethical Obligations**

  Current behavior and classroom performance demonstrate adherence to the ethical expectations and obligations of professional practice, noted in the NASW Code of Ethics and the Code of Ethics for Social Work Licensure in Pennsylvania. Ethical behaviors include:

  o Adherence to the NASW Code of Ethics and the Code of Ethics for Social Work Licensure in PA.

  o Disclose history of charges and/or convictions of an offense that is contrary to professional practice.

  o Systematic evaluation of clients and their situations in an unbiased, factual way.

  o Suspension of personal biases during interactions with others.

  o Comprehension of another individual's way of life and values.

  o Empathic communication and support of the client as a basis for a productive professional relationship.

  o Appreciation of the value of diversity.

  o Effective and non-judgmental relation to and work with others who are different from oneself.

  o Appropriate service to all persons in need of assistance, regardless of the person's age, class, race, religious beliefs, gender, disability, sexual orientation, and/or value system.

  o No imposition of personal, religious, sexual and/or cultural values on clients.

  o Demonstration of respect for the rights of others.

  o Commitment to client's rights to freedom of choice and self-determination.

o Maintenance of confidentiality as it relates to human service, classroom activities, and field placement.

o Demonstration of honesty and integrity by being truthful about background, experiences, and qualifications; doing one's own work; giving credit for the ideas of others; and providing proper citation of source materials.

o Demonstration of clear, appropriate, and culturally sensitive boundaries. Does not sexually harass others; make verbal or physical threats; become involved in sexual relationships with clients, supervisors, or faculty; abuse others in physical, emotional, verbal, or sexual ways; or participate in dual relationships where conflicts of interest may exist.

Appendix B
Online Resources

College Teaching Positions

Academic360.com
www.academic360.com/
Lists available faculty positions by discipline.

AcademicKeys.com
www.academickeys.com/
Job searches and a listing of "Who's Who" in various disciplines and academic resources.

CollegeGrad.com
www.collegegrad.com/college/college-teaching-jobs.shtml
A site that lists entry-level positions for recent graduates.

EducationAmerica.net
www.educationamerica.net/
Includes overseas teaching positions.

HigherEdJobs.com
www.higheredjobs.com/

Expert Advice on Teaching College

Here are just a few of the Web sites out there that offer a wide array of tips on teaching college.

Arizona State University, The Center for Learning and
Teaching Excellence
http://clte.asu.edu

Higher Education
www.highereducation.org

Honolulu Community College
http://honolulu.hawaii.edu

The National Teaching and Learning Forum
www.ntlf.com

New York University, Center for Teaching Excellence
www.nyu.edu/cte

University of Maryland, Center for Teaching Excellence
www.cte.umd.edu

Glossary of Terms

Active learning – Students understand concepts and can apply them to different scenarios, rather than simply remembering them.

Adjunct professor – A part-time college professor.

Adult learner – A mature student, often one who has returned to college after dropping out or to continue their education.

Assessment – A test or other measurement that determines if students learned what was taught.

Assistant teachers – Graduate students who work as part-time instructors at their college or university.

Blog – A Web site where professors can list course-related information and interact with students and other teachers.

Clickers – A remote control device that allows students to feed responses to classroom questions into a computer.

Critical thinking – The ability to analyze information from various sources and understand how the information ties together.

Discrimination – Treating someone unfairly because he or she is a minority.

Distance learning – Using video cameras or the Internet to bring a presentation into the classroom from a remote location.

Faculty – College staff members.

Group discussions – Small groups of students that are formed to discuss and debate an issue or solve a problem.

Internship – An experience, often in a workplace, that allows students to gain real-world experience in their chosen fields of study.

Knowledge – Understanding the facts, truths, or principles relating to a certain subject.

Lecture – A verbal presentation before a classroom.

Mentors – Experienced teachers who guide new teachers.

Motivation – A drive that inspires someone to achieve a goal.

Multimedia – The use of sound, film, video, and other media in the classroom.

Objective – What a course intends to accomplish.

Outcome – What students will be able to perform following a course.

Plagiarism – Passing off another's ideas as one's one, either intentionally or not. This can lead to punishment or removal from a college.

Rubric – A definition of what constitutes high and low levels of student performance.

Stereotype – A predetermined generalization about a person or a group of people.

Syllabus – A written summary of the requirements, topics studied, time-line, and expectations for a course.

Tenure-track – Full-time teachers who, after fulfilling certain requirements, achieve a status that protects them from being dismissed without cause or due process.

Textbook – A book that includes information covered in a course.

Bibliography

Bain, Ken (2004). *What the Best College Teachers Do*. Cambridge, Massachusetts and London, England: Harvard University Press.

Cutting, Ed (2008, August 29). Are Students Customers? Yes. *National Association of Scholars*. Retreived from <**http://www.nas.org/polArticles.cfm?doc_id=319**>

Filene, Peter (2005). *The Joy of Teaching, A Practical Guide for New College Instructors*. Peter Filene.

Fredericks, Anthony D. (2007). *The Complete Idiot's Guide to Teaching College*. Alpha Books: The Penguin Group.

Handling Improper Interview Questions. Adapted from an article in the December 2007 *NACE Journal*, by Nancy Conrad and Tanya Salgado. **http://www.jobweb.com/interviews.aspx?id=1343**.

Graves, Lucia (2008, October 3). Which Types of Students Cheat Most? *U.S.News & World Report*. Retrieved from **www.usnews.com.**

Gray, Paul & Drew, David E. (2008). *What They Didn't Teach You in Graduate School: 199 Helpful Hints for Success in Your Academic Career.* Stylus Publishing, LLC.

Lang, James M. (2008). *On Course: A Week-By-Week Guide to Your First Semester of College.* Cambridge, Massachusetts and London, England: Harvard University Press.

Lieberg, Carolyn (2008). *Teaching Your First College Class: A Practical Guide for New Faculty and Graduate Student Instructors.* Stylus Publishing.

Students Use Clickers to Help Guide College Lessons. (2005, May 5). Retrieved from **http://abcnews.go.com/Technology/DyeHard/story?id=727409&page=.**

Students Who Use 'Clickers' Score Better on Physics Tests. (2008, July 18). Retrieved from **http://www.sciencedaily.com/releases/2008/07/080717092033.htm**.

Author Biography

Terry Webster covered education issues in major news markets across the country for more than 15 years. During that time, she interviewed hundreds of administrators, teachers, and students on a wide range of issues. A lifelong learner, Webster is fascinated by the many lessons life teaches us both inside and outside the classroom.

Index

Q

Questionnaire, 288, 199, 202

Quiz, 280-281, 288-289, 291, 91-92, 186, 197

R

References, 279-281, 40, 45-46, 212, 228

Reputation, 53, 70, 155

Résumé, 40-45, 47, 213, 243, 247

Role-playing, 106, 119, 124

Rubric, 280, 175, 303

S

Salary, 23, 29, 35, 39, 55-57

Schedule, 285, 20, 30, 33, 61, 67, 69, 87, 92, 94, 172, 187, 236, 254

Self-evaluation, 142, 207

Shy, 88, 95, 145, 150

Social Networking, 78, 80, 243

Stereotype, 158, 303

Survey, 288, 93, 199, 202, 227

T

Tardiness, 68

Teaching Contract, 55

Teamwork, 81, 126

Tenure, 34, 55-61, 210, 235, 238, 245-247, 249-252, 254, 256, 17

Textbook, 67, 73-76, 89, 137, 145, 303

Tuition, 71, 167

U

U.S. Bureau of Labor, 35

V

Video, 79, 84, 90-92, 95, 142, 224, 243, 302

Violence, 114-115, 182, 192, 215, 220-221